The HAPPY WARRIOR

THE LIFE STORY OF
SIR WINSTON CHURCHILL
as told through Great Britain's *EAGLE* comic of the 1950s

The HAPPY WARRIOR

THE LIFE STORY OF
SIR WINSTON CHURCHILL
as told through Great Britain's *EAGLE* comic of the 1950s

COMMENTARY BY RICHARD M LANGWORTH CBE

UNIFORM
PRESS

Uniform Press, an Imprint of Unicorn Press Ltd

66 Charlotte Street
London W1T 4QE
www.unicornpress.org

ISBN 9 781906 50990 3

This edition published by Unicorn Press 2014

Design by Anna Hopwood/ahdesign

Printed in India by Imprint Digital Ltd.

CONTENTS

THE EAGLE THAT DARED

COLIN FREWIN remembers vividly what Fridays meant as a young lad growing up in post-war Britain.

'Every Friday was a big Friday,' Frewin recalls. 'It's when we learned of the next episode of Dan Dare's adventures. What would he do next?'

Throughout Britain, from 1950 to 1969, thousands of youngsters like Frewin would race to their local newsagents every Friday, pence in hand and sometimes parents in tow, to buy their latest issue of the *Eagle* comic, featuring the adventures of Dan Dare, Pilot of the Future.

But this was no ordinary comic strip. This was something the likes of which the country – in fact, the world – had never seen.

Each issue of the *Eagle* was chockablock with adventures for boys. There was news on the Eagle Club that all readers were invited to join (60,000 of them did by the second issue).

Plus the latest adventures of Extra Special Agent Harris Tweed, and of Terry Walls and other characters as well as Dan Dare. Tips from the pros on boxing and jiu-jitsu, and instructions on how to keep a goldfish. A hobbies corner ('collecting cheese labels' was one). And frequently, a photo competition or word game.

You could order a complete mint set of British Colonial stamps ('please tell your parents you are ordering'). Or send in the box tops from the Sugar Puffs cereal to get the miniature plastic cowboy and Indian FREE!

If you were very good, and had done a kind or heroic deed, your teacher or family might suggest you for the Mug of the Month distinction, which earned you a write-up with your photo.

Then in the centre were those amazing cutaway diagrams of trains and planes and aircraft carriers that were as detailed as an engineer's. And even the back cover, something there – another adventure! This time of real action heroes, Montgomery or Nelson or Churchill. All those pages – 16, at least! All that fantastic colour! Best of all, all theirs.

The *Eagle* belonged not to their parents or their teachers (though both, for reasons we shall discover, heartily approved of it), but to them – to Frewin and his mates and thousands of English boys like them. Even the editor's note inside was addressed to them. And so for this new generation of Britons, Fridays spilled over into Saturdays and then Sundays, clusters of boys gathered together to share in the adventures of an exciting new age.

All of which owed its start to a parish priest in England's northwest county of Lancashire.

Reverend Marcus Morris, the vicar of St. James's Church in the seacoast town of Southport, saw a need, and then an opportunity, for comics with a conscience. He believed that the youth of 1950s Britain needed a publication that inculcated standards and morals as it entertained with action and adventure.

The *Eagle* was not hatched overnight. Its genesis followed a twisting, sometimes torturous path. It eventually took the Oxford-educated vicar to

London and, after a suitable number of rejections, to Hulton Press on Fleet Street.

What made the *Eagle* soar above other comic strips of the time was its quality – the paper, the printing, the colour, the writing and, most especially, the art. Frank Hampson was the co-founder of the comic and the head artist of Dan Dare and other *Eagle* action heroes. His first studio was a converted bakery in Southport. In a 1974 interview (Hampson died in 1985), he said of Dan Dare: 'I wanted to give [young people] something that made the future more hopeful.' He also had a hunch that space travel would launch in the not-too-distant future.

'They were so different from the comics we had been used to,' says Paul Courtenay, a retired officer of the British Army who remembers 'avidly' reading the weekly adventures as a teenager. 'The others were all rubbish. The *Eagle* was a breath of fresh air.' And it signaled a headwind of a larger magnitude.

'It was a new Elizabethan age in Britain,' explains Frewin, who today is the Chief Executive of the Dan Dare Corporation and the owner of the *Eagle* comic. 'We had come out of the war and had a new young queen and new horizons to explore.'

The *Eagle* was itself a feat of derring-do. It captured, celebrated, and at times uncannily presaged Britain's technological dexterity in the realms of aviation, defence, and architecture. The trains, boats, planes, and buildings that appeared as the centre cutaways of each issue were more than fanciful designs. They were based on actual models that Hampson and his team had created. They were also extraordinarily well detailed. In fact, the cutaway of a nuclear submarine revealed its inner workings so splendidly that the Admiralty demanded to know the source of such precision.

As Frewin says, 'It was based on existing reports of the submarine, plus a little imagination and guesswork as to how things would work.'

What the creators of the *Eagle* probably could not have imagined was just how well their idea would work.

Whatever else happened in the world on 14 April 1950, there was this: the first issue of the *Eagle* hit the newsagents in England and sold 900,000 copies. The Pilot of the Future had rocketed to fame.

Readers were encouraged to clip the reminder that was printed, coupon-fashion, on the editor's page and to take it to their newsagents, asking them to order the *Eagle* for them every week. Eventually the *Eagle* would produce offspring – first *Girl*, then *Robin* and *Swift* – so that girls and younger siblings could have their own publications as well.

The *Eagle* maintained its high-flying trajectory, selling three-quarters of a million copies on average each week. Dan Dare would soon even have his own radio show, broadcast on Radio Luxembourg.

Even the Pilot of the Future could not know about a twenty-first-century phenomenon called social networking, but that's exactly what the *Eagle* created. In its own, pre-Internet way, it formed a virtual forum for young boys. Plus it had the blessings of Mum and Dad and the headmaster.

When, for instance, readers asked where the title 'The Happy Warrior' came from for the Churchill series, Reverend Morris told his young readers that it was from a poem by Wordsworth. He encouraged them to have their teachers help them find it. 'It is well worth reading,' he advised.

'It was a thrill,' says Frewin, summing up that Friday frisson of *Eagle* excitement. 'Youngsters were as dazzled as their parents. My father would read the issues after I did.'

Frewin's father had been a pilot in the Royal Air Force during World War II. When Winston Churchill died in 1965, he took his son to the funeral. 'We queued for eight hours to go past the coffin,' Frewin says. He was only four when the *Eagle* debuted 'The Happy Warrior,' the Weekly back-cover chronicle of Churchill's life that ran from 4 October 1957 to 6 September 1958. Those covers are reproduced in this work in their entirety, exactly as they appeared in the original editions, just the way Frewin first read them at the age of eight. (His father had kept all the back issues of *Eagle*, a custom that fathers and sons all over England happily hewed to.)

'The Greatest EAGLE News Yet!' was the advance notice that 'The Happy Warrior' received, because Churchill was, proclaimed the *Eagle*, 'the most famous man in the world.' Readers were again advised to alert their local newsagents, as without a reserved copy they may be out of luck. The estimable Frank Bellamy drew the series, which debuted in Volume 8, Number 40.

'On the one cover was this fictitious hero, Dan Dare. On the other was this real hero, Winston Churchill,' says Frewin. It seems a fitting pairing.

The cover of the issue of 4th October 1957, featuring the first installment of 'The Happy Warrior'

Frewin describes Dan Dare as 'a superhero with old-fashioned values.' He was a twentieth-century vision of the future, with morals firmly rooted in the century past – rather like the real hero named Churchill.

Although the original *Eagle* ceased publication in 1969, its legacy lives on in unexpected places. Some of the young lads studying those cutaways became England's new crop of architects and engineers. In their work can be seen the stamp of an *Eagle*. In the *Eagle*, in turn, can be seen a precursor of today's graphic novel.

Perhaps its greatest legacy resides in the minds and hearts of those thousands of youngsters who pored over its pages, and in the contributions to country and community they went on to make.

In the very first issue of *Eagle*, on the editor's page, Marcus Morris issued his *Eagle* Club 'manifesto' Members of the club would…

a) *Enjoy life and help others to enjoy life. They will not enjoy themselves at the expense of others.*
b) *Make the best of themselves. They will develop themselves in body, mind and spirit. They will tackle things for themselves and not wait for others to do things for them.*
c) *Work with others for the good of all around them.*
d) *Always lend a hand to those in need of help. They will not shirk difficult or dangerous jobs.*

It would be nice to think that such adventures will go on forever - that, like the last panel of so many pages of the *Eagle*, it is a story to be continued.

THE LION STILL ROARS

Richard M Langworth CBE

WHAT may strike a seasoned Churchill reader about 'The Happy Warrior' is how unlikely it would be for such a comic to appear today however factual the story it tells.

We live in an iconoclastic age. Values, traditions, and legacies once held sacred are questioned, plumbed, and deconstructed by self-appointed analysts and would-be philosophers. It's unlikely that today anyone would publish a comic commemorating, in purely hagiographic terms, any real-life leader, even Winston Churchill.

William Manchester called the habit of viewing past times through a modern prism 'generational chauvinism': the gratuitous assumption that only today's generation is capable of understanding and eradicating 'the mess of centuries.' Those were in fact the words Clement Attlee, Britain's postwar prime minister, used in 1951 to describe the task before his government. Churchill, then Leader of the Opposition, objected:

The mess of centuries – that is all we were. The remark is instructive because it reveals with painful clarity [Attlee's] point of view and sense of proportion. Nothing happened that was any good until they came into office. We may leave out the great struggles and achievements of the past - Magna Carta, the Bill of Rights, Parliamentary institutions, Constitutional Monarchy, the building of our Empire – all these were part of the mess of centuries … But at last a giant and a Titan appeared to clear up the mess of centuries. Alas, he cries, he has had only six years to do it in. [1]

As Churchill's experience demonstrates, people were decrying the 'struggles and achievements of the past'

long before today; but the mutterings have grown to a cacophony amplified by a 24/7 news media and that digital Hyde Park Corner, the World Wide Web.

'The Happy Warrior,' first published fifty years ago, had no truck with any of this. Nor was it surprising. In the 1950s, World War II was as recent as the presidential election of Bill Clinton is today. Nobody had yet published a seriously critical work on the wartime prime minister who had led a Britain alone against Hitler's Third Reich. Even though the effort rendered Britain bankrupt, and postwar governments did little to revive it, Churchill was still a hero to most citizens, every young person, and, of course, the publishers of the *Eagle*.

Valid criticism is part of the historical process, and the advent of questioning works, which began with Field Marshal Alanbrooke's diaries in 1959, was perfectly understandable. Churchill lived a long life and made many mistakes. His successes outweighed his failures, but as a noted scholar of his domestic politics says, 'To me it only serves to diminish Churchill to regard him as super-human.' [2]

But in 1958, basking in retirement, having just published at age 84 the fourth and final volume of his magisterial *History of the English-Speaking Peoples*, Churchill seemed super-human. It's astonishing that he has managed to scale the intervening half century with his reputation still intact, after so many complaints, some of them deserved.

The only hints of criticism in 'The Happy Warrior' are the suggestion that Winston traded his English for another boy's Latin at school (4 Oct.) and that it was foolhardy – which it probably was – to defend

Crete in World War II (9 May). The shoals on which Churchill briefly went aground – the gold standard and General Strike in the 1920s, die-hard opposition to the India Bill and Gandhi in the early 1930s, over-zealous support of Edward VIII in the 1936 abdication crisis – are all untouched by this account. Of course, it is a war story, not a biography, so successes like settling the Middle East in 1921 or helping write the Irish Treaty in 1922 are similarly omitted.

But even militarily, 'The Happy Warrior' is almost universally positive. Churchill is not tagged with the failed Dardanelles expedition, nor any of his lesser controversies in World War I.[3] Unremarked in World War II are his underestimation of German tank tactics (resulting in the fall of France – not that this was his fault) and his confidence in Stalin at Teheran and Yalta (resulting in the Cold War). The fall of Singapore and loss of two capital ships (the battleship HMS *Prince of Wales* and the battlecruiser HMS *Renown*) to Japanese aircraft are mentioned, but without blaming Churchill (23 May).

The comic strip does convey Churchill's surprise at the speed of France's collapse in 1940 and the fall of Tobruk in 1942. Author Clifford Makins missed a wonderful line about Tobruk, when Churchill learned of its loss on a visit to Washington: 'I am the most miserable Englishman in America since Burgoyne' – the British general defeated at Saratoga during the American Revolution.[4] Another famous loss line came in 1945, when his wife said the lost election was a blessing in disguise (23 Aug): 'At the moment,' Churchill replied, 'it appears quite effectively disguised.'[5]

The comic strip is remarkably accurate on Winston's youth, given what was known at the time – mostly his own writings. In the 1950s, the vast trove of the Churchill Archives at Cambridge was not yet organized, and would not begin to be deeply plumbed by the faithful biographer, Martin Gilbert, for nearly a decade after 'The Happy Warrior' was

published. There was no evidence, for example, that Churchill's Harrow Latin was much better than he claimed; the Latin paper containing only his name and an ink blot (4 Oct.) has never surfaced in school archives. Nevertheless, 'The Happy Warrior' goes a good way to emphasize the now-certain fact that Winston at school was much better than he himself claimed in his famous autobiography.[6]

His years as a dashing young officer eager to see action are also well covered, even if artist Frank Bellamy gives him a build resembling that of Chuck Norris. Young Churchill was more accurately described by the 'dead or alive' Wanted Poster a Boer official drafted in 1899: 'Englishman, 25 years old, about 5 ft. 8 in. tall, indifferent build, walks with a forward stoop, pale appearance, red-brownish hair, small and hardly noticeable moustache, talks through his nose and cannot pronounce the letter 'S' properly'.[7]

His early battles in Queen Victoria's 'little wars' are forthrightly described. Fifty years later, one regrets that space precluded some of Churchill's characteristically magnanimous tributes to the fallen foe at Omdurman: '...as brave men as ever walked the earth. The conviction was borne in on me that their claim beyond the grave in respect of a valiant death was not less good than that which any of our countrymen could make.'[8]

The Anglo-Boer War of 1899-1902 and his sensational escape from Boer captivity are well and clearly treated. There was no room for amplifications, which would blunt the charges that fly around about his racism, which was no more than the gratuitous attitude of his generation. In fact, Churchill had remarkably enlightened ideas for a Victorian, typified by his comments following an argument with a racist guard at the Boer prison over black South Africans: 'What is the true and original root of Dutch aversion to British rule? ...It is the abiding fear and hatred of the movement that seeks to place the native on a level with the white man ... The dominant race is to be deprived of their superiority; nor is a tigress robbed of her cubs more furious than is the Boer at this prospect.' [9]

The comic skips quickly over Churchill's radical decade when, as a rising young Conservative-turned-Liberal, he took office following the great Liberal landslide of 1906 and fought with Lloyd George for social reform and the welfare state; and when he married Clementine Hozier, the greatest and most beneficent influence over him for the rest of his life (31 Jan.).

Then, suddenly, the Guns of August fire.

The World War I treatment is uncritical but good, and Bellamy's faces are remarkably lifelike. We meet Prime Minister H.H. Asquith, whose lack of decisive leadership doomed the Dardanelles campaign, and eventually his premiership. And Lord Kitchener (31 Jan.), who promises 'an assault on Gallipoli by the Army' but in fact failed promptly to send ground troops. And Admiral 'Jacky' Fisher, at first more enthusiastic than Churchill about the Dardanelles, but who then changed his mind and resigned, taking Churchill with him in the Cabinet crisis that followed.

'The Happy Warrior' has no room to explain the personal impact of Churchill's resignation, which Clementine vividly recalled: 'When he left the Admiralty he thought he was finished. I thought he would never get over the Dardanelles. I thought he would die of grief.' [10]

A comic strip has to concentrate on essentials and cannot always be 100 percent faithful to the actual words spoken. When Churchill resigned from the government and went to fight in Flanders, Asquith never said to him, 'What a waste! You're throwing your career away!' (14 Feb.) Personally Asquith was glad to see him go. The comic is accurate on Churchill's close call in the field, leaving his headquarters moments before it was shattered by German shells (21 Feb.), but inaccurate in suggesting

that his Army colleagues told him to return to Parliament. (He really needed no urging.) But for a man in his forties to go off to fight in that desperate war was a revealing testimony to his courage, and here the comic has him exactly right.

The period between the two world wars is covered in a page, and Adolf Hitler makes his baleful appearance in the run-up to World War II (7 Mar.). The 1930s, when Churchill's lone voice signaled the terror to come, is the period for which he is most revered by many who study him. Unfortunately he plays this role in only one pane, and the quotation is necessarily truncated. Readers may wish to contemplate the full passage, delivered in 1932, seventy days before Hitler took power:

Now the demand is that Germany should be allowed to re-arm. Do not delude yourselves. Do not let His Majesty's Government believe – I am sure they do not believe – that all that Germany is asking for is equal status . . . That is not what Germany is seeking. All these bands of sturdy Teutonic youths, marching through the streets and roads of Germany, with the light of desire in their eyes to suffer for their Fatherland, are not looking for status. They are looking for weapons, and, when they have the weapons, believe me they will then ask for the return of lost territories and lost colonies, and when that demand is made it cannot fail to shake and possibly shatter to their foundations every one of the countries I have mentioned, and some other countries I have not mentioned. [11]

Churchill's urgent warnings during the 1930s encompass some of the finest passages in the English language. The greatest of them all came six months before Munich:

I have watched this famous island descending incontinently, fecklessly, the stairway which leads to a dark gulf. It is a fine broad stairway at the beginning, but after a bit the carpet ends. A little farther on there are only flagstones, and a little farther on still these break beneath your feet . . . if mortal catastrophe should overtake the British Nation and the British Empire, historians a thousand years hence will still be baffled by the mystery of our affairs. They will never understand how it was that a victorious nation, with everything in hand, suffered themselves to be brought low, and to cast away all that they had gained by measureless sacrifice and absolute victory – gone with the wind! [12]

It is no wonder that Bellamy drew Hitler as a crazed monster. But Hitler was a perceptive fanatic, who judged his opponents shrewdly, and half his military decisions were correct. Fortunately there was the other half. Contrary to the comic strip, for example, Hitler did not expect the D-Day invasion at Normandy (12 July); he expected it at Calais, and disposed his troops accordingly.

Nor did Hitler say, 'We will conquer Europe, Asia, the world . . . now for Poland, France and England!' (7 Mar.) The reader should be aware that Hitler's aspirations were not global, not at least in 1940. Yet he had made it plain what he did want, and that was frightening enough.

What Churchill knew, and his detractors didn't, was that a Britain coexistent with a Nazi continent was unacceptable, for national if not for moral reasons:

You must have diplomatic and correct relations, but there can never be friendship between the British democracy and the Nazi power, that power which spurns Christian ethics, which cheers its onward course by a barbarous paganism, which vaunts the spirit of aggression and conquest, which derives strength and perverted pleasure from persecution, and uses, as we have seen, with pitiless brutality the threat of murderous force. That power cannot ever be the trusted friend of the British democracy. What I find unendurable is the sense of our country falling into the power, into the orbit and influence of Nazi Germany .... I foresee and foretell that the policy of submission will carry with it restrictions upon the freedom of speech and debate in Parliament, on public platforms, and

discussions in the Press, for it will be said - indeed, I hear it said sometimes now - ordinary, common English politicians. Then, with a Press under control, in part direct but more potently indirect, with every organ of public opinion now-that we cannot allow the Nazi system of dictatorship to be criticised by chloroformed into acquiescence, we shall be conducted along further stages of direct but more potently indirect, with every organ of public opinion doped and our journey.' [13]

Some scholars argue that had he died in 1939, Churchill would be regarded as a minor, brilliant failure. Really? Wouldn't his reputation have depended on how World War II had turned out? Besides, that doesn't take into account his massive historical and biographical Writings, his role in World War I, and his reforms as a fighting Liberal.

Few ever argued that there was anyone else to lead the country in May 1940. Absent Churchill, who? This comic was produced, of course, in glorious hindsight, but the reader should consider what Churchill's daughter Mary often says: 'Remember – nobody knew in those days whether we were going to win.'

Win they did, and as befits a tribute to national greatness, 'The Happy Warrior' is replete with characters famous in those days, loved and unloved. There is Captain Bernard Warburton-Lee of HMS *Hardy*, who led the attack on Narvik, Norway and who, mortally wounded, gave the signal: 'Continue to engage the enemy.' (14 Mar.) There is French General Maxime Weygand (Bellamy makes him unmistakable even from the rear). When Churchill asks, 'Ou est la masse de manoeuvre?,' Weygand replies fatefully: 'Aucune. There is none.' (28 Mar.) We see Max Beaverbrook, who truly did 'Work miracles with the aircraft industry.' (18 Apr.) 'Some people take drugs,' Churchill once said, 'I take Max.' [14] There are admirals and generals, the capable and the incompetent, all faithfully brought back to life by Makins and Bellamy.

Field Marshal Alanbrooke, Chief of the Imperial General Staff, whose 1959 diaries were the first serious criticism of Churchill's leadership, is cast almost as if Makins read his book in advance. 'Brookie' seems always to pose statements that Churchill rebuffs, although in fact Churchill never countermanded his Chiefs of Staff, and Alanbrooke did not say they could not conquer ltaly before invading France (12 July). Field Marshal Bernard Montgomery, who brings victory in North Africa, gets his just due (13 June). It is nowhere recorded that Churchill remarked about Montgomery, 'In defeat, indomitable; in victory, insufferable' – though it's possible the thought crossed his mind. General Sir Harold Alexander, that quiet giant, is frequently pictured. His telegram, after completing his mission in early 1943, was memorable . . .

Sir: The Orders you gave me on August 15, 1942, have been fulfilled. His Majesty's enemies, together with their impedimenta, have been completely eliminated from Egypt, Cyrenaica, Libya, and Tripolitania. I now await your further instructions. [15]

. . . as was Churchill's equally famous reply: 'Well, obviously, we shall have to think of something else . . .'

Churchillian readers will love the way Clifford Makins captures Churchill's best ripostes. When Weygand asks what he will do when the Germans 'swarm across the Channel,' Churchill replies (as indeed witnesses heard him say): 'Drown as many as possible [of them on the way over] – and as for the others, when they crawl ashore we will *frapper sur la tête!*' (4 Apr.) In an age when many British schoolchildren knew some French, Makins saw no need to translate 'knock them on the head.'

President Roosevelt, who appears at the Atlantic Charter meeting in August 1940 and is engulfed by Pearl Harbor on the same page (23 May), is handled diplomatically. It would have been impolitic, two years after the United States had resisted and ultimately scuttled the Franco-British-Israeli Suez campaign, to fling epithets toward dead American presidents. And after all, America and Russia had won the war that Britain in her most sublime hour didn't lose. So nothing is said of Roosevelt's uneven handling of Churchill, enthusiastically co-signing the Atlantic Charter while resisting any drift toward war, until Pearl Harbor finally forced the issue.

This was a good editorial decision: Roosevelt was as widely admired as Churchill in Britain, maybe more so, and his contributions to the war effort had been prodigious. Hence Churchill's tribute herein, which is a little garbled (16 Aug). His actual words were: 'For us, it remains only to say that in Franklin Roosevelt there died the greatest American friend we have ever known, and the greatest champion of freedom who has ever brought help and comfort from the new world to the old.' [16]

Stalin's heated confrontations with Churchill and his angry accusation that the British were afraid of fighting Germans (13 June) are frankly recounted, and Churchill's response is likewise documented. Makins was less careful about offending Russians: the reader learns five installments later, in a handsome presentation of the invasion of Europe by Anglo-American-Canadian forces on June 6, 1944, that Stalin was wrong. And a page later, we are shown the horror of the flying bombs Hitler loosed on London, in the second great blitz of the War (26 July).

We witness Victory in Europe Day, May 8, 1945, almost as a coda to the story, and here the canny Frank Bellamy may have missed one of the most dramatic scenes of the War: Churchill waving to the crowds from the Ministry of Health in Whitehall, shouting into the microphone, 'God bless you all.'

Lest works like 'The Happy Warrior' be too devoted to his own persona, Churchill himself made sure that his countrymen received the thanks. He expresses that here (23 Aug), but more eloquently perhaps in 1954 when, honored by Parliament on his eightieth birthday, he said of the British people:

Their will was resolute and remorseless, and as it proved, unconquerable. It fell to me to express it, and if I found the right words you must remember that I have always earned my living by my pen and by my tongue. It was a nation and race dwelling all round the globe that had the lion heart. I had the luck to be called upon to give the roar. I also hope that I sometimes suggested to the lion the right places to use his claws. [17]

V-E Day is the end of our story. 'The Happy Warrior' makes no attempt to discuss the rest of the war, perhaps because Churchill was no longer in charge. More surprisingly but possibly because they were recent and contentious topics, there is also nothing about his 1946 'Iron Curtain' speech warning of Soviet ambitions; of his second premiership, when the vision of nuclear extinction sent him on a failed quest for peace with the Russians; or of his bittersweet postwar relations with Eisenhower over summit meetings, decolonization, and Suez. Those were recent events in 1958, and perhaps too painful; the *Eagle* was in the business of defining heroes.

What can we make of this half-century-old tribute? The story is accurately told, the figures remarkably true to life. But it is only part of the Churchill story and should not lead the reader to think he was strictly a man of war.

Churchill concluded early in life that 'the story of the human race is war,' and – at least before the advent of nuclear weapons – regarded wars as recurring phenomena. Because he always urged fighting with 'might and main' he is often regarded purely as a warrior. It is less well known that he tried to stop the First World War, and the Second. Some authors have even truncated his quotations to make him fit their vision of a war enthusiast. Here is one unedited quotation that makes clear his true attitude:

Much as war attracts me and fascinates my mind with its tremendous situations – I feel more deeply every year – and can measure the feeling here in the midst

of arms – what vile and wicked folly and barbarism it all is. [18]

Another point one draws from the narrative is more positive: for the vast majority of free peoples, what 'The Happy Warrior' says is still accepted, and probably always will be. In 1995 the late William Buckley, in an unforgettable speech, gave the best rationale for this work when he said:

Mr. Churchill had struggled to diminish totalitarian rule in Europe, which however increased. He fought to save the Empire, which dissolved. He fought socialism, which prevailed. He struggled to defeat Hitler, and he won. It is not I think the significance of that victory, mighty and glorious though it was, that causes the name of Churchill to make the blood run a little faster. He subsequently spoke diffidently about his role in the war, saying that the lion was the people of England, that he had served mainly to provide the roar. But it is the roar that we hear when we pronounce his name; it is simply mistaken that battles are necessarily more important than the words that summon men to arms or who remember the call to arms. The Battle of Agincourt was long forgotten as a geopolitical event, but the words of Henry V with Shakespeare to recall them, are imperishable in the mind, even as which side won the Battle of Gettysburg will dim from the memory of men and women who will never forget the words spoken about that battle by Abraham Lincoln. The genius of Churchill was his union of affinities of the heart and of the mind, the total fusion of animal and spiritual energy. [19]

One is left only to wonder how the Happy Warrior himself saw this comic upon its publication – for he was alive and sentient, and such things usually were brought to his attention. One may imagine him as his daughter did, sitting in his garden chair at Chartwell, strategically among the foliage, watching the butterflies as they fluttered over the buddleia he had planted for them. [20] Though he was growing old thinking he had not accomplished very much in the end, 'The Happy Warrior' might have given him pause.

It was William Buckley's proposal that Churchill's words were 'indispensable to the benediction of that hour,' Britain's finest, whatever the glories that came before or the disappointments that came after.

It is no coincidence that our view of Churchill is still more or less that of Clifford Makins and Frank Bellamy fifty years ago. For those who remember, or are willing to learn, Winston Churchill is still the Happy Warrior.

NOTES

1. Winston S. Churchill, Woodford, Essex, 12 October 1951. Robert Rhodes James, ed. *Winston S.Churchill: His Complete Speeches 1897-1963*, vol. 8 (New York: Bowker, 1974), 8263.

2. Prof. Paul Addison, University of Edinburgh, author of *Churchill on the Home Front* (1992), in *Finest Hour* 127 (summer 2005): 6.

3. Current scholarship holds Churchill much less to blame for the Dardanelles fiasco than twentieth-century opinion; indeed, he had preferred a Baltic flanking attack, though he did go all-out for the Dardanelles once the plan was agreed on.

4. Kay Halle, *Irrepressible Churchill* (New York and Cleveland: World, 1966), 200.

5. Winston S. Churchill, *The Second World War*, vol. 6, *Triumph and Tragedy* (London: Cassell, 1954), 583.

6. Winston S. Churchill, *My Early Life: A Roving Commission* (London: Thornton Butterworth; New York: Charles Scribner's Sons, 1930), 15-57.

7. Ephesian [C.E. Bechhofer Roberts], *Winston Churchill*, 3rd ed. (London: George Newnes, 1936), 74.

8. Winston S. Churchill, *The River War, vol. 2* (London: Longmans Green, 1899), 221.

9. Winston S. Churchill, *London to Ladysmith via Pretoria* (London: Longmans Green, 1900), 134-35.

10. Martin Gilbert, *Churchill: A Life* (London: Heinemann, 1991), 321.

11. House of Commons, 23 November 1932. Rhodes James, *Complete Speeches*, vol. 5, 5199-5200.

12. Winston S. Churchill, *Arms and the Covenant* (London: George Harrap, 1938), 465. Not in House of Commons transcripts; the passage was likely added by Churchill to his book.

13. House of Commons, 5 October 1938. Winston S. Churchill, *Blood, Sweat and Tears* (Toronto: McClelland 8: Stewart, 1941), 76-77.

14. Circa 1941. Sir John Colville to the author, 1985.

15. House of Commons, 11 February 1943. Rhodes James, *Complete Speeches*, vol. 7, 6752.

16. House of Commons, 17 April 1945. Rhodes James, *Complete Speeches*, vol. 7, 7141.

17. House of Commons, 30 November 1954. Rhodes James, *Complete Speeches*, vol. 8, 8608-09.

18. Churchill to his wife, 15 September 1909. In *Randolph S. Churchill, Winston S. Churchill, Companion Volume II, Part 2* (London: Heinemann, 1967), 912.

19. William F. Buckley Jr., 'Let Us Now Praise Famous Men,' 12th International Churchill Conference, Boston, 27 October 1995. *Churchill Proceedings 1994-1995* (Hopkinton, N.H.: The Churchill Centre, 1998), 81-82.

20. Mary Soames, 120th Birthday Celebration, Naval and Military Club, London, 29 November 1994.

BEGINNING TODAY!

The HAPPY WARRIOR

The true life story of
SIR WINSTON CHURCHILL

WINSTON CHURCHILL WAS BORN AT BLENHEIM PALACE ON THE 30th NOVEMBER, 1874.

TOLD BY CLIFFORD MAKINS
DRAWN BY FRANK BELLAMY

YOUNG WINSTON LOVED READING...

..AND PLAYING WITH TOY SOLDIERS.

WOULD YOU LIKE TO BE A SOLDIER, BOY?

OH YES, PAPA!

YOU SHALL, MY BOY, YOU SHALL.

WHEN HE WAS 12, WINSTON SAT FOR THE ENTRANCE EXAMINATION FOR HARROW.

THE LATIN PAPER! OH DEAR!

WINSTON DID NOT DO VERY WELL

CHURCHILL'S LATIN IS NOT UP TO MUCH! NEVER MIND, WE WILL PUT HIM IN THE BOTTOM FORM, AND HOPE FOR THE BEST.

BUT WINSTON WAS VERY GOOD AT ENGLISH, WHICH HE ADORED.

WELL DONE, CHURCHILL. A SPLENDID EFFORT.

WINSTON SOON FOUND A WAY ROUND THE PROBLEM OF LATIN!

IF YOU TELL ME MY LATIN TRANSLATIONS, I WILL WRITE YOUR ENGLISH ESSAYS.

WHAT A SPLENDID IDEA!

CONTINUED

The HAPPY WARRIOR

Winston Churchill was born in 1874. He went to school at Harrow, where he was only an average scholar, although he excelled at English. While stagnating in the lowest form, Churchill won a prize open to the whole school, reciting 1,200 lines of Macaulay's *Lays of Ancient Rome* . . .

TOLD BY CLIFFORD MAKINS
DRAWN BY FRANK BELLAMY

LARS PORSENA OF CLUSIUM BY THE NINE GODS HE SWORE !

WELL DONE, CHURCHILL ! A FIRST RATE PERFORMANCE !

WINSTON LOVED SINGING THE FAMOUS SCHOOL SONGS OF HARROW . . .

. . . AND HE WON THE PUBLIC SCHOOL CHAMPIONSHIP IN FENCING !

When Winston left Harrow, he passed into Sandhurst – after three tries ! At the end of his course, he was placed eighth out of 150. In 1895, he was gazetted to the 4th Hussars, a famous cavalry regiment stationed at Aldershot . . .

WINSTON SOON BECAME AN EXPERT HORSEMAN — LEARNING THE HARD WAY !

CHURCHILL LONGED TO SEE ACTION AND LISTENED SPELLBOUND TO THE YARNS OF HIS COMMANDER, COLONEL BRABAZON.

BARNES, THERE'S A WAR IN CUBA. WE MIGHT HAVE A LOOK AT IT. WHAT D'YOU THINK ?

I'M GAME, CHURCHILL.

SPLENDID ! WE HAVE THE COLONEL'S BLESSING, AND HERE ARE THE PAPERS FROM THE SPANISH AUTHORITIES.

IN 1895, CHURCHILL AND BARNES SAILED TO NEW YORK AND FROM THENCE TO HAVANA . . .

CUBA ! HOW EXCITING— HOW MYSTERIOUS !

WHERE ARE THE ENEMY ?

HERE, THERE AND EVERYWHERE ! IF YOU WANT TO SEE FIGHTING, YOU MUST JOIN A MOBILE COLUMN !

WINSTON JOINED A SPANISH COLUMN WHICH WAS HUNTING CUBAN REBELS . . .

AH, ACTION AT LAST !

CONTINUED

15

The HAPPY WARRIOR

Winston Churchill – born in the year 1874 – went to Harrow School, and then on to Sandhurst, where he did well. In 1895, Churchill was gazetted to the 4th Hussars, a famous cavalry regiment, at that time stationed at Aldershot – but love of adventure and longing for action soon took Winston, together with a fellow subaltern, to Cuba, where the Spaniards were fighting a war against rebels . . .

TOLD BY CLIFFORD MAKINS
DRAWN BY FRANK BELLAMY

THE REBELS HAVE RUN DEEP INTO THE JUNGLE. WE CANNOT FOLLOW THEM THERE.

THAT WAS A PRETTY POOR SCRAP!

MAYBE — BUT IT WAS REAL — IT WAS EXCITING! DID YOU HEAR THOSE BULLETS SMITING THE TREES?

SOON AFTER, THE TWO SUBALTERNS LEFT CUBA.

GOODBYE, CUBA — HOME TO ENGLAND!

WINSTON RETURNED TO HIS REGIMENT AT ALDERSHOT...

WHAT SPLENDID NEWS!

WELCOME BACK, CHURCHILL! IN SIX MONTHS, THE REGIMENT SAILS FOR INDIA.

Winston spent six months' leave in English society and, during this period, he met many famous men of the day. Among them was General Sir Bindon Blood, hero of campaigns on the turbulent Indian frontier . . .

SIR! WHEN YOU LEAD YOUR NEXT EXPEDITION IN INDIA, I BEG YOU TO LET ME COME.

ALL RIGHT — THAT'S A PROMISE!

IN AUTUMN 1896 WINSTON'S REGIMENT SAILED TO BOMBAY

WINSTON AND HIS FRIENDS, BARNES AND BARING, SHARED A FINE BUNGALOW AT THE BANGALORE GARRISON.

HERE IS OUR HOUSE, GENTLEMEN! LET US MAKE OURSELVES AT HOME!

IN INDIA, CHURCHILL WAS A POLO FANATIC...

...AND A GREAT READER.

Later, when tribesmen rose on the North-West Frontier, Sir Bindon Blood led a force against them. Winston immediately set off to join him, both in the capacity of a soldier, and as correspondent for the Indian *Pioneer* and the British *Daily Telegraph*.

TWO THOUSAND MILES AND FIVE DAYS' TRAVEL TO THE FRONTIER. WHAT A JOURNEY!

I'LL GET THERE! GOODBYE!

SIX DAYS LATER, WINSTON REACHED THE FRONT AT THE MALAKAND PASS...

LT. CHURCHILL REPORTING TO GENERAL SIR BINDON BLOOD!

CONTINUED

The HAPPY WARRIOR

The true life story of SIR WINSTON CHURCHILL

Lt. Winston Churchill – born in 1874 – has obtained leave from his regiment at Bangalore and gone to the North-West Frontier, where Pathan tribesmen are in revolt. He has gone as both soldier and journalist at the invitation of General Sir Bindon Blood, who is leading the Malakand Field Force. After journeying by train and tonga, Winston – covered in dust – arrives at the frontier …

TOLD BY CLIFFORD MAKINS
DRAWN BY FRANK BELLAMY

THE GENERAL'S LEADING A COLUMN AGAINST THE BUNERWALS. WHEN HE GETS BACK, WE'LL ALL BE ON THE MOVE.

SOME DAYS LATER, THE MALAKAND FIELD FORCE BEGAN ITS LONG TREK THROUGH THE MOUNTAIN VALLEYS.

THEN SIR BINDON BLOOD SUMMONED WINSTON …

OUR 2ND. BRIGADE IS GOING INTO THE MAMUND VALLEY. IT WILL BE A FIERCE SCRAP ALL RIGHT. YOU CAN JOIN THEM IF YOU LIKE !

YES, SIR. AT ONCE !

WINSTON RODE INTO THE VALLEY WITH THE CAVALRY AT THE HEAD OF THE BRIGADE.

SEVERAL HOURS LATER…

HERE, TAKE MY HORSE. I'M GOING ON WITH THE INFANTRY.

THE VILLAGE IS DESERTED, AND THE HILLS SEEM AS QUIET AS THE GRAVE.

I WOULDN'T RELY ON THAT !

SUDDENLY THE HILLS SWARMED WITH HOSTILE TRIBESMEN…

ACTION ! THIS IS MORE LIKE IT !

RETREAT AT ONCE ! WE'LL COVER YOU FROM THE REAR !

AH !

DEADLY FIRE HALTED WINSTON'S RETREATING PARTY.

GET THE WOUNDED ! DRAG THEM AWAY ! QUICKLY !

CONTINUED

The HAPPY WARRIOR

The true life story of SIR WINSTON CHURCHILL

India, 1896. Lt. Winston Churchill has gone to the North-West Frontier to join the Malakand Field Force which is fighting rebel tribesmen. He joins a brigade which advances into the Mamund Valley and soon finds himself engaged in a desperate action with a small company of men. Under withering fire, the company retreats down a hill with its wounded . . .

TOLD BY CLIFFORD MAKINS
DRAWN BY FRANK BELLAMY

PRESS ON WITH THE WOUNDED. I'LL KEEP THE SAVAGES AT BAY!

AIEE!

WINSTON ALONE FACED THE FIERCE PATHAN TRIBESMEN.

MISSED, MY FINE FRIEND! NOW YOU ARE FOR IT!

THE TRIBESMAN FELL BEHIND A ROCK!

STILL MORE OF THEM! I MUST MAKE FOR COVER!

AS WINSTON DASHES OVER THE ROCKS, THE BULLETS WHINE AROUND HIM.

SPLENDID WORK!

TO THE BOTTOM OF THE HILL WITH THE WOUNDED! HURRY!

WINSTON FIRED SHOT AFTER SHOT AS THE COMPANY STRUGGLED DOWN THE HILL.

COURAGE, MEN! WE'RE NEARLY THERE!

CONTINUED

The HAPPY WARRIOR

The true life story of
SIR WINSTON CHURCHILL

In 1896, Lt. Winston Churchill is on the Indian North-West Frontier with the Malakand Field Force which is fighting rebel tribesmen. Winston takes part in a spirited action in the Mamund Valley. His company is hard pressed and suffers heavy casualties, but with great dash and courage Winston conducts a fighting retreat to the British lines.

TOLD BY CLIFFORD MAKINS
DRAWN BY FRANK BELLAMY

HURRAH! WE'VE MADE THE LINES.

WINSTON BROUGHT THE COMPANY SAFELY HOME!

BUT THE FRENZIED TRIBESMEN SURGED ON!

FIRE!

THEY'RE ON THE RUN!

THE TRIBESMEN'S MAD RUSH WAS HALTED JUST IN TIME. THEY FLED IN DISORDER.

PHEW! THAT WAS WARM WORK!

SPLENDID FELLOW!

WINSTON RETURNS TO BANGALORE.

WINSTON'S BACK!

HERE HE COMES!

YOU'VE CERTAINLY HAD A FIRST RATE WAR, WINSTON!

I HAVE — AND NOW I'M GOING TO WRITE A BOOK ABOUT IT!

AND SO THE TIRELESS WINSTON WROTE A BOOK ABOUT HIS ADVENTURES CALLED 'THE MALAKAND FIELD FORCE'.

When Winston's book was published it was well received and praised by the Prince of Wales and the Prime Minister, Lord Salisbury. But Winston craved action again. On leave in England, he had news that Sir Herbert Kitchener's army was advancing against the Dervishes in the Sudan.

I WANT TO FIGHT IN THE SUDAN CAMPAIGN. DO YOU THINK THE PRIME MINISTER WOULD PUT IN A WORD FOR ME?

CERTAINLY! I'LL ASK HIM RIGHT AWAY.

LATER...

THE PRIME MINISTER HAS SENT A WIRE TO KITCHENER.

WONDERFUL!

BUT THE NEXT DAY...

BAD NEWS, WINSTON—KITCHENER HAS WIRED BACK 'NO'. HE HAS ALL THE OFFICERS HE REQUIRES.

THAT'S A BLOW! BUT I REFUSE TO BE BEATEN!

CONTINUED

The HAPPY WARRIOR

After fighting on the Indian North-West Frontier, Lt. Winston Churchill returns to England on leave. He tries to attach himself to Sir Herbert Kitchener's army which is marching against the Dervishes in the Sudan. But although the Prime Minister puts in a word for Winston, Kitchener wires his refusal. Winston talks with his friend, Sir Schomberg M'Donnell...

TOLD BY CLIFFORD MAKINS
DRAWN BY FRANK BELLAMY

I MUST GET TO THE SUDAN! I'LL ASK LADY ST. HELIER. SHE'S A GREAT FRIEND OF THE ADJUTANT-GENERAL, SIR EVELYN WOOD!

GOOD FOR YOU, WINSTON!

WINSTON WASTED NO TIME...

I ADMIRE YOUR SPIRIT, WINSTON. I WILL SPEAK TO THE ADJUTANT GENERAL MYSELF.

MA'AM, I AM GREATLY OBLIGED TO YOU.

A FEW DAYS LATER...

A LETTER FROM THE WAR OFFICE! HURRAH! I'VE BEEN POSTED TO EGYPT. I SHALL JUST BE IN TIME FOR THE BATTLE!

GOODBYE, MOTHER!

THE NEXT DAY, WINSTON'S MOTHER WAVED HIM GOODBYE!

SIX DAYS LATER, HE JOINED THE 21st LANCERS IN CAIRO...

WELL, MR CHURCHILL — YOU MUST HAVE PULLED A FEW STRINGS TO GET HERE!

YES, SIR. I WONDER WHAT KITCHENER THINKS OF THIS!

AUGUST 27th, 1898. KITCHENER'S ARMIES SWARMED ACROSS THE NILE...

THAT'S THE LOT — ALL SAFELY ACROSS.

AND STILL NO SIGN OF THE ENEMY.

WE'RE ON THE MOVE! OUR SQUADRON WILL SUPPORT THE ADVANCED PATROLS.

ALL RIGHT, MEN — HERE WE GO!

MR CHURCHILL! THE ENEMY IS SEVEN MILES AWAY AND ADVANCING — RIDE AT ONCE TO KITCHENER AND TELL HIM!

I'M OFF, SIR!

CONTINUED

EAGLE 22 *November* 1957

The HAPPY WARRIOR

The true life story of
SIR WINSTON CHURCHILL

WHAT A SPLENDID SIGHT! AH, THERE IS KITCHENER — RIDING AT THE HEAD!

1898. Lt. Winston Churchill has been attached to the 21st Lancers for the Sudan Campaign where British and Egyptian armies, under Sir Herbert Kitchener, are fighting the Dervishes. On the eve of the Battle of Omdurman, Winston gallops to the Commander-in-Chief to report the enemy's positions. After six miles hard riding he sights the allied armies from a hill . . .

TOLD BY CLIFFORD MAKINS
DRAWN BY FRANK BELLAMY

SIR, I AM REPORTING FROM THE 21st LANCERS. THE ENEMY IS ABOUT SEVEN MILES AWAY AND ADVANCING STEADILY.

PHEW! I HOPE MY INFORMATION IS CORRECT! NOW I MUST REJOIN MY SQUADRON!

I HAVE INFORMED KITCHENER OF THE SITUATION.

GOOD! BUT NOW THE DERVISH ADVANCE HAS STOPPED, WE WILL HAVE OUR BATTLE TOMORROW!

NEXT DAY THE TWO ARMIES CLASHED...

THE BATTLE IS ON. SOON IT WILL BE OUR TURN.

THE ENEMY'S ATTACK HAS BEEN REPULSED.

NOW WE MUST KEEP THEM ON THE RUN. PREPARE TO ADVANCE.

THE 21st LANCERS CHARGED INTO BATTLE.

NOW THEN!

NO SWORD FOR ME! THE PISTOL IS MY BEST FRIEND!

IT'S DEATH OR GLORY NOW!

CONTINUED

The HAPPY WARRIOR

The true life story of
SIR WINSTON CHURCHILL

Lt. Winston Churchill is attached to the 21st Lancers, who form part of Kitchener's army in the Sudan. It is 2nd September, 1898, and, on the sandy plain before the city of Omdurman, the great battle with the Dervish hordes has begun. Soon, with Winston leading his troops, the 21st Lancers charge towards the enemy . . .

TOLD BY CLIFFORD MAKINS
DRAWN BY FRANK BELLAMY

RIDE STRAIGHT THROUGH THE ENEMY!

SOON WINSTON WAS IN THE THICK OF IT!

AH!

AND ANOTHER!

I MUST BREAK THROUGH HERE OR I SHALL BE CUT TO PIECES!

WELL DONE, SIR! I THOUGHT YOU'D NEVER MAKE IT!

NEVER SAY DIE!

WE HAVEN'T LOST MANY MEN, BUT... LOOK OUT, SIR!

I THINK I HAVE ONE SHOT LEFT...

NOW WE SHALL SEE!

CONTINUED

The HAPPY WARRIOR

On the great desert plain of the Nile, the Battle of Omdurman is being fought. The Dervish hordes have been repelled by intense fire from the British-Egyptian armies, under Sir Herbert Kitchener. Lt. Winston Churchill, with the 21st Lancers, leads his troop in a rousing Cavalry charge. As the troop reforms, a savage bursts into the ranks with a spear and rushes straight towards Winston.

TOLD BY CLIFFORD MAKINS
DRAWN BY FRANK BELLAMY

JUST IN TIME — AND THAT WAS MY LAST SHOT!

WHAT CASUALTIES HAVE WE SUFFERED, SERGEANT?

FOUR MEN MISSING, SIR, AND SEVERAL OTHERS WOUNDED. NOT SO BAD!

WE MUST PREPARE TO CHARGE AGAIN ON COMMAND — AH, HERE COMES THE SQUADRON LEADER!

RIDE BACK TO THE ENEMY'S FLANK AND HALT! WE'LL TREAT THEM TO SOME GUN-FIRE NOW.

RIGHT, SIR! FORWARD!

DISMOUNT — AND GET INTO LINE!

KEEP UP YOUR FIRE! THEY'RE RETREATING!

IT'S ALL OVER, SERGEANT. THE BATTLE IS OURS!

YES, SIR. THAT WAS QUITE A SCRAP!

THE BATTLE OF OMDURMAN WAS OVER. WINSTON SAILED BACK UP THE NILE TO CAIRO.

WELL, THAT WAS A QUICK WAR AND NO MISTAKE.

GOOD OLD WINSTON — ESCAPED WITHOUT A SCRATCH AS USUAL!

HERE COMES WINSTON BACK FROM THE WARS!

BRAVO!

AND NOW WHAT ARE YOU GOING TO DO, WINSTON?

WRITE ANOTHER BOOK, WIN THE INDIAN POLO TOURNAMENT, GO INTO POLITICS AND FIGHT IN ANY WAR THAT COMES ALONG!

CONTINUED

EAGLE 13 December 1957

The HAPPY WARRIOR

The true life story of SIR WINSTON CHURCHILL

Attached to the 21st Lancers in the Sudan, Lt. Winston Churchill fights in the battle of Omdurman against the Dervishes, and distinguishes himself in an historic cavalry charge on the banks of the Nile. Then, the war won, he returns to London, where he is welcomed in society.

TOLD BY CLIFFORD MAKINS
DRAWN BY FRANK BELLAMY

GOODBYE! WHEN SHALL WE SEE YOU AGAIN?

NEXT SPRING I HOPE. AFTER THE POLO TOURNAMENT, I SHALL LEAVE THE ARMY AND LIVE IN LONDON.

Winston went to India and helped his regiment win the Polo Tournament of 1899. Resigning his commission, he came home to England, where, after contesting Oldham unsuccessfully for the Tories, he settled down to write his book 'The River War'. But then...

MR OLIVER BORTHWICK OF THE MORNING POST TO SEE YOU, SIR.

THANK YOU. SHOW HIM IN.

OLIVER!

WINSTON! THE BOER REPUBLICS HAVE ISSUED AN ULTIMATUM TO OUR FORCES IN SOUTH AFRICA. WAR IS IMMINENT. WILL YOU ACT AS PRINCIPAL WAR CORRESPONDENT FOR THE MORNING POST?

WHEN DO I START?

IMMEDIATELY! YOU SAIL ON THE NEXT BOAT!

I WISH THIS SHIP WOULD GET A MOVE ON. BY THE TIME WE REACH THE CAPE THE WAR WILL BE OVER!

THE BOERS ARE BESIEGING LADYSMITH AND MAFEKING IN NATAL PROVINCE.

THAT'S THE PLACE FOR ME!

WINSTON WENT TO THE FRONT LINE AT ESTCOURT IN NATAL AND MET AN OLD FRIEND...

CHURCHILL!

HALDANE!

I'M TAKING AN ARMOURED TRAIN ON RECONNAISSANCE! CARE TO COME ALONG?

LIKE A SHOT!

HERE WE ARE, WINSTON. HOP IN!

I THINK WE SHOULD PUT ON A SHOW FOR YOU, WINSTON!

I HOPE SO. MUSTN'T DISAPPOINT THE READERS OF THE MORNING POST!

CONTINUED

24

The HAPPY WARRIOR

The true life story of SIR WINSTON CHURCHILL

War has broken out between the British and the Boers in South Africa. Lt. Winston Churchill has hurried to the front as principal war correspondent of the Morning Post. At Estcourt, in Natal, he meets a friend, Captain Haldane, and accompanies him on reconnaissance in an armoured train . . .

TOLD BY CLIFFORD MAKINS
DRAWN BY FRANK BELLAMY

WE'LL STOP HERE A MOMENT, WINSTON, AND TELEGRAPH OUR POSITION TO HEADQUARTERS.

RIGHT!

LOOK, HALDANE! ON THE HILL!

THE HILL BEHIND THE TRAIN WAS SWARMING WITH ENEMY TROOPS!

IT'S THE BOERS! THEY'RE CUTTING US OFF. FULL STEAM BACK TO H.Q., OR WE SHALL LOSE TROOPS, TRAIN AND ALL!

WE'RE PASSING THE BOERS NOW!

WAIT FOR IT!

FIRE!

THE TRAIN GOT THE FULL FURY OF THE ENEMY FIRE.

HALDANE! I THINK WE ... AH!

THE TRAIN STOPPED – VIOLENTLY!

IF YOUR CHAPS KEEP FIRING, I'LL NIP OUT AND SEE WHAT'S HAPPENED TO THE TRAIN!

RIGHT, CHURCHILL!

GOOD LORD – WHAT A MESS!

CONTINUED

The HAPPY WARRIOR

The true life story of
SIR WINSTON CHURCHILL

Winston Churchill has gone to South Africa as correspondent for the Morning Post to report the war between Britain and the Boer Republics. He goes on reconnaissance with an armoured train in Natal Province. Without warning, the train is attacked by Boers and derailed. Winston, braving enemy fire, runs towards the head of the train . . .

TOLD BY CLIFFORD MAKINS
DRAWN BY FRANK BELLAMY

WE MUST CLEAR THE LINE AND GET THE TRAIN ON THE MOVE — AH, THERE'S THE ENGINE DRIVER!

HE'S RUNNING AWAY! HI! COME BACK HERE!

HANDS OFF! LET ME GO! I'M NOT RISKING MY LIFE ANY MORE.

YOU'RE DOING A GREAT JOB! BACK YOU GO — AND WAIT FOR ORDERS.

WINSTON PERSUADED THE ENGINE DRIVER TO RETURN TO HIS CAB.

STAND CLEAR! I'M GOING TO DRIVE THE ENGINE FULL TILT TO TRY TO CLEAR THE LINE!

QUICK, DRIVER! LET IT RIP!

THE ENGINE PUSHED THE WRECKAGE FROM THE LINE.

ALL ABOARD — QUICK AS YOU CAN!

THERE'S THE BRIDGE. ONCE ACROSS THE GORGE WE CAN TAKE STOCK OF THE SITUATION.

STOP THE TRAIN! THE REST OF THE TROOP ARE FALLING BEHIND. I'LL GO BACK AND HURRY THEM ON.

AH! THERE THEY ARE.

NO! YE GODS — IT'S THE BOERS!

TO BE CONTINUED

The HAPPY WARRIOR

The true life story of **SIR WINSTON CHURCHILL**

November, 1899. The Boer War has broken out in South Africa and Lt. Winston Churchill is reporting the campaign for the Morning Post. At the front, in Natal Province, Winston goes on reconnaissance in an armoured train which is ambushed by the Boers, and derailed. Winston takes charge of the operations and frees the engine from the wreckage. He then leaves the engine and goes to rally the British soldiers trailing behind, but is trapped by the Boers himself.

TOLD BY CLIFFORD MAKINS
DRAWN BY FRANK BELLAMY

THE BOERS — I'M TRAPPED!

DESPERATELY, WINSTON SCRAMBLED UP THE BANK AT THE SIDE OF THE TRACK...

I'VE SHAKEN THEM OFF BUT I CAN'T STAY HERE! THE RIVER'S NOT FAR AWAY — I'LL MAKE A DASH FOR IT.

BUT WHEN WINSTON STOOD UP...

HALT! STAY WHERE YOU ARE!

I'VE NO OPTION. PERHAPS I CAN GET HIM BEFORE HE GETS ME!

MY PISTOL — IT'S GONE!

NOTHING TO DO BUT SURRENDER.

CROSS THE LINE — QUICKLY!

THERE ARE THE REST OF YOUR FRIENDS — ALL PRISONERS!

TAKE THIS MAN AND STAND HIM APART FROM THE OTHERS. WE'LL DEAL WITH HIM IN A MOMENT!

WAR CORRESPONDENTS WHO TAKE PART IN THE FIGHT ARE USUALLY SHOT.

THIS LOOKS LIKE THE END FOR ME!

TO BE CONTINUED

The HAPPY WARRIOR

The true life story of
SIR WINSTON CHURCHILL

Winston Churchill, aged 25, and principal war correspondent of the Morning Post, is reporting the Boer War in South Africa. He goes on reconnaissance with a party of troops in an armoured train and, after taking an active part in a fierce fight, is taken prisoner. He is placed apart from the other prisoners and stands in the pouring rain, expecting to be shot!

TOLD BY CLIFFORD MAKINS
DRAWN BY FRANK BELLAMY

CHEER UP! IF WE DECIDE TO SHOOT YOU WE'LL GIVE YOU A DECENT BURIAL!

THANKS VERY MUCH!

AH, THEY'VE MADE THEIR DECISION. YOU'LL KNOW YOUR FATE IN A MINUTE.

YOU CAN COME ALONG WITH THE OTHER PRISONERS, CHURCHILL. WE DON'T CATCH THE SON OF A LORD EVERY DAY!

COME ON! STEP IT OUT, THERE — ONLY ANOTHER FIFTY MILES TO GO!

EVENTUALLY WINSTON ARRIVED AT THE PRISON-CAMP FOR OFFICERS IN PRETORIA.

WELL HERE WE ARE — PRISON AT LAST!

THANK GOODNESS – I'M DEAD BEAT!

ONE MONTH LATER.

I'M GOING TO GET OUT OF THIS PLACE EVEN IF I DIE IN THE ATTEMPT!

IT'S CERTAINLY OUR DUTY TO ESCAPE IF WE CAN.

MY MIND'S MADE UP. I SHALL TRY TO GIVE THE SENTRIES THE SLIP AND JUMP OVER THE WALL — TONIGHT!

AND THAT EVENING, IN CIVILIAN CLOTHING, WINSTON AWAITED HIS OPPORTUNITY...

IF ONLY THOSE TWO SENTRIES WOULD HAVE A CHAT TOGETHER, I'D STAND A CHANCE!

GOOD! NOW'S THE TIME!

AS THE SENTRIES ENJOYED A SMOKE WINSTON SLIPPED OVER THE FENCE.

DONE IT!

TO BE CONTINUED

The HAPPY WARRIOR

The true life story of
SIR WINSTON CHURCHILL

While reporting the Boer War in South Africa, Lt. Winston Churchill takes part in a reconnaissance on an armoured train. He distinguishes himself, but is captured and taken to an officers' prison camp at Pretoria. Determined to escape, he makes his attempt in bright moonlight and scales the wall of the prison compound without being seen . . .

TOLD BY CLIFFORD MAKINS
DRAWN BY FRANK BELLAMY

I'M FREE —AND NO SOUND OF AN ALARM.

ANOTHER SENTRY! WELL, CAN'T TURN BACK NOW—MUST RISK IT!

RIGHT UNDER HIS NOSE —AND NOT A CHALLENGE!

Outside Pretoria, Winston jumped a train. At daybreak he left the train and spent the day hiding in a wood. At night he waited for another train, but none came. In despair, he left the railway line . . .

PHEW! THE GOING'S TOUGH! I'M JUST ABOUT ALL IN!

HOURS LATER . . .

A COAL MINE — I'LL STOP HERE AND TRY TO BLUFF MY WAY THROUGH.

WHO IS IT? WHAT DO YOU WANT?

I NEED HELP. I'VE HAD AN ACCIDENT.

I'VE FALLEN OFF A TRAIN AND I THINK I'VE DISLOCATED MY SHOULDER.

COME IN THEN.

NOW WHO ARE YOU AND WHERE DO YOU COME FROM? AND I'D LIKE TO KNOW THE TRUTH!

RIGHT, I WILL TELL YOU THE TRUTH. I AM WINSTON CHURCHILL, WAR-CORRESPONDENT OF THE MORNING POST. LAST NIGHT I ESCAPED FROM PRETORIA AND I AM MAKING MY WAY TO THE FRONTIER.

DON'T MOVE AND KEEP QUIET!

NOW I'M DONE FOR!

I'M GLAD TO KNOW YOU MR CHURCHILL. THANK GOD YOU STUMBLED ACROSS THIS PLACE. WE ARE ALL BRITISH HERE AND WILL SEE YOU THROUGH!

TO BE CONTINUED

The HAPPY WARRIOR

The true life story of **SIR WINSTON CHURCHILL**

Lt. Winston Churchill, war correspondent of the Morning Post, is taken prisoner while reporting the Boer War in South Africa. He escapes from the prison camp at Pretoria and after hours of wandering over the veldt seeks shelter at a coal mine. Luckily, the manager is an Englishman and promises to help Winston on his way.

TOLD BY CLIFFORD MAKINS
DRAWN BY FRANK BELLAMY

THE BOERS ARE LOOKING EVERYWHERE FOR YOU. THEY WERE HERE THIS AFTERNOON. BUT DON'T WORRY — SIT DOWN AND I'LL GET YOU SOME FOOD.

THANK YOU — I'M FAMISHED!

LATER...

FINISHED YOUR MEAL? GOOD! COME ON, MR CHURCHILL, I'VE SPOKEN TO THE MEN AND WE'RE GOING TO HIDE YOU DOWN THE PIT.

HERE ARE SOME CANDLES. YOU'LL BE QUITE SAFE HERE, BUT DON'T MOVE WHATEVER HAPPENS. WE WON'T FORGET YOU!

THIS IS HARDLY HOME FROM HOME BUT IT'S BETTER THAN PRISON. I'LL SOON BE OUT OF HERE, PLEASE GOD, AND BACK IN THE FRAY AGAIN.

After six days in the mine, while Boers hunted him overhead, Winston was stowed away on a goods train bound for Portuguese East Africa. Soon he reached his goal and strolled through the streets of Lourenco Marques.

THE BRITISH CONSULATE — WHAT A BLESSED SIGHT!

I WANT TO SEE THE CONSUL.

BE OFF WITH YOU! IF YOU HAVE ANY BUSINESS WITH THE CONSUL CALL TOMORROW MORNING AT NINE!

YOU GO TO BLAZES! I WANT TO SEE THE CONSUL RIGHT AWAY! RIGHT NOW!

WHAT ON EARTH IS THE MATTER? I AM THE CONSUL.

AND I AM WINSTON CHURCHILL — ESCAPED FROM THE BOERS!

WINSTON CHURCHILL! WELCOME, MY DEAR CHAP — YOU'RE A HERO!

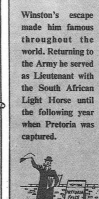

Winston's escape made him famous throughout the world. Returning to the Army he served as Lieutenant with the South African Light Horse until the following year when Pretoria was captured.

WELL, CHURCHILL, THE WAR'S NEARLY OVER. WHAT ARE YOUR PLANS NOW?

I'VE RESIGNED MY COMMISSION AND AM RETURNING TO ENGLAND. I HEAR THERE'S A GENERAL ELECTION IN THE OFFING.

TO BE CONTINUED

The HAPPY WARRIOR

Winston Churchill, taken prisoner while reporting the Boer War in South Africa, escapes from a prison camp at Pretoria and, after many hazards, reaches safety in Portuguese East Africa. He then joins the South African Light Horse but with the end of the war in sight, Winston resigns his commission.

**TOLD BY CLIFFORD MAKINS
DRAWN BY FRANK BELLAMY**

I AM GOING HOME TO TRY MY HAND AT POLITICS AGAIN. I THINK I STAND A FAIR CHANCE THIS TIME.

FAIR CHANCE! I SHOULD SAY SO!

YOU'LL BE THE HERO OF THE HOUR!

A REMARKABLE CHAP YOUNG CHURCHILL — BUT A BIT RASH FOR POLITICS I THINK.

HM, WE MUST WAIT AND SEE.

Winston returned in triumph to England. In the general election of 1900 he was returned as Conservative member for Oldham. Two years later, he joined the Liberal party. He married Miss Clementine Hozier in 1908, and became Home Secretary in 1910. In 1914 he was appointed First Lord of the Admiralty.

WAR WITH GERMANY IS IMMINENT. THE FLEET MUST BE MOBILIZED AT ONCE.

BUT, SIR, THE SANCTION OF THE CABINET...

THERE'S NO TIME TO WAIT FOR THE CABINET'S SANCTION. THE FLEET MUST TAKE UP ITS WAR STATIONS — NOW!

WHITEHALL, AUGUST 4th, 1914...

WAR

THIS DISPATCH TO ALL BRITISH SHIPS AND NAVAL ESTABLISHMENTS THROUGHOUT THE WORLD — 'COMMENCE HOSTILITIES AGAINST GERMANY'.

JANUARY, 1915...

THE PRIME MINISTER MR ASQUITH, THE ARMY CHIEF LORD KITCHENER AND WINSTON CHURCHILL HELD A COUNCIL OF WAR...

A NAVAL EXPEDITION AGAINST THE DARDANELLES.

WE HAVE REACHED DEADLOCK ON THE WESTERN FRONT. OUR RUSSIAN ALLIES ARE PRESSING FOR ACTION AGAINST TURKEY. WHAT CAN BE DONE?

TO BE FOLLOWED BY AN ASSAULT ON GALLIPOLI BY THE ARMY.

NEXT MONTH THE OPERATION BEGAN...

WEEKS LATER...

WE HAVE POUNDED AWAY FOR WEEKS AND LOST THREE BATTLE SHIPS. OUR NAVAL OPERATION MUST STOP. WE MUST TELL THE CABINET THAT IT IS THE ARMY'S TURN NOW.

BACK IN WHITEHALL...

YOU HAVE SEEN THE TELEGRAMS FROM ADMIRAL DE ROBECK. BEYOND DOUBT WE MUST TELL HIM TO CARRY ON OUR NAVAL OPERATIONS.

I DON'T AGREE. HE'S THE MAN ON THE SPOT AND WE MUST TRUST HIS JUDGMENT.

I AGREE WITH YOU, FISHER!

NO, CHURCHILL — I'M AFRAID WE MUST STOP IT.

PRIME MINISTER — WE MUST SUSTAIN OUR NAVAL ACTION AT THE DARDANELLES.

TO BE CONTINUED

The HAPPY WARRIOR

The First World War is raging. Winston Churchill, First Lord of the Admiralty, is at odds with some of his colleagues over the Naval operations against the Turks at the Dardanelles. The Admiralty Board, with Lord Fisher prominent, think that the Fleet should stop action for a while. Winston disagrees. He goes to the Prime Minister, Mr Asquith, and tries in vain to enlist his support.

TOLD BY CLIFFORD MAKINS
DRAWN BY FRANK BELLAMY

I'M SORRY, CHURCHILL — I CANNOT OVERRULE THE ADMIRALTY BOARD. NAVAL OPERATIONS AT THE DARDANELLES MUST STOP. IT IS THE ARMY'S TURN NOW.

PRIME MINISTER, THE ARMY IS NOT YET READY TO ASSAULT THE BEACHES. THE DELAY MAY PROVE FATAL!

A MONTH LATER BRITISH TROOPS LANDED ON THE GALLIPOLI PENINSULAR IN FACE OF TERRIFIC FIRE FROM THE TURKS.

BLIMEY, THIS IS WORSE THAN BRIGHTON BEACH!

WE SHOULD HAVE JOINED THE NAVY, MATE!

MEANWHILE, ANOTHER BATTLE RAGED IN WHITEHALL.....

STILL WE KEEP A VAST FLEET AT THE DARDANELLES — WAITING TO BE SUNK BY GERMAN SUBMARINES!

LORD FISHER, SERVICE CHIEF OF THE NAVY, CONTINUALLY OPPOSED CHURCHILL'S STRATEGY.

OUR ARMIES ARE FIGHTING FOR THEIR LIVES WITH THEIR BACKS TO THE SEA. THEY MUST BE PROTECTED, LORD FISHER!

I HAVE OPPOSED THIS CAMPAIGN FROM THE START. WE SHOULD HAVE GONE TO THE BALTIC!

A FEW DAYS LATER...

HAVE YOU SEEN THE FIRST LORD? I MUST FIND HIM!

WHY YES — THERE HE IS, WALKING ACROSS THE HORSEGUARDS.

SIR! LORD FISHER HAS RESIGNED!

SO BE IT! NOW I MUST GO TO THE PRIME MINISTER.

PRIME MINISTER, HERE IS THE LIST OF NAMES CONTAINING A SUCCESSOR TO LORD FISHER AND A NEW ADMIRALTY BOARD.

I CANNOT ACCEPT IT. IN VIEW OF THE CRISIS I HAVE DECIDED TO FORM A NEW GOVERNMENT. I'M AFRAID THERE WILL BE NO PLACE FOR YOU AT THE ADMIRALTY.

EXCUSE ME, SIR! I HAVE AN URGENT MESSAGE FOR MR CHURCHILL TO RETURN AT ONCE TO THE ADMIRALTY.

NOW WHAT'S THE MATTER?

SIR! WE HAVE NEWS THAT THE GERMAN HIGH SEAS FLEET HAS PUT TO SEA!

NOW'S OUR CHANCE!

TO BE CONTINUED

The HAPPY WARRIOR

The true life story of
SIR WINSTON CHURCHILL

May, 1915. Winston Churchill, First Lord of the Admiralty, has been asked to resign when the Prime Minister forms a coalition government following a split between Churchill and Lord Fisher over the control of the Dardanelles campaign. Suddenly there is news that the German Fleet has put to sea. At the Admiralty, The first Lord hopes for a victorious naval action.

TOLD BY CLIFFORD MAKINS
DRAWN BY FRANK BELLAMY

GET THE CHIEF OF STAFF AND THE SECOND SEA LORD. WE MUST MEET THE GERMAN FLEET WITHOUT DELAY AND DESTROY IT.

THE GRAND FLEET IS TO PREPARE FOR SEA AT ONCE. ALSO LIGHT CRUISERS, DESTROYERS AND SUBMARINES – EVERY AVAILABLE VESSEL MUST BE USED.

NOW FOR THE WAITING! IF THERE IS A BATTLE AND WE WIN – THE WAR WILL BE SHORTENED AND MANY LIVES SAVED.

THE GERMAN FLEET HAS ALTERED COURSE AND IS BOUND FOR HOME. THERE IS NO HOPE OF ENGAGING THEM.

NEXT MORNING...

WHAT A CRUSHING BLOW!

Churchill was forced to resign. In the new government his office was Chancellor of the Duchy, and his special job was to help with the planning of the Gallipoli campaign. But it was too late.

ON THE BEACHES AT GALLIPOLI, THE FIGHT GREW FIERCER STILL.

THEY'RE ALL DEAD.

NO – THIS ONE'S STILL BREATHING!

STRETCHER PARTY!

CASUALTIES ARE MOUNTING AT A TERRIFIC RATE. WE MUST HAVE MORE MEN.

OUR REINFORCEMENTS ALWAYS ARRIVE TOO LATE – WE DON'T STAND A CHANCE!

IN THE AUTUMN OF 1915 GALLIPOLI WAS EVACUATED.

BACK TO BLIGHTY!

AND ABOUT TIME TOO!

AND IN LONDON...

I SPY OUR EX-FIRST LORD OVER THERE.

OUR MOST BRILLIANT FAILURE! WE HAVE HEARD THE LAST OF HIM I RECKON!

WINSTON, I HEAR RUMOURS THAT YOU INTEND TO RESIGN YOUR OFFICE.

THAT IS RIGHT. I'M TAKING A COMMISSION IN THE OXFORDSHIRE YEOMANRY AND SHALL GO TO FRANCE.

WHAT A WASTE! YOU'RE THROWING YOUR CAREER AWAY!

OTHER MEN ARE RUNNING THE WAR NOW AND I AM OUT OF IT. THAT I CAN'T STAND!

AND SO MAJOR WINSTON CHURCHILL WENT TO FRANCE.

TO BE CONTINUED.

The HAPPY WARRIOR

The true life story of **SIR WINSTON CHURCHILL**

The First World War – November, 1915. Soon after losing his job as First Lord of the Admiralty, Winston Churchill left the political arena and joined the Army. He was commissioned as Major in the Oxfordshire Yeomanry, and without delay crossed the Channel to France.

TOLD BY CLIFFORD MAKINS
DRAWN BY FRANK BELLAMY

MAJOR CHURCHILL, SIR JOHN FRENCH WANTS TO SEE YOU AT G.H.Q.—A CAR IS WAITING.

CHURCHILL WAS DRIVEN TO THE HEADQUARTERS OF THE BRITISH COMMANDER-IN-CHIEF, SIR JOHN FRENCH.

BEFORE I TAKE A COMMAND, SIR JOHN, I SHOULD LIKE SOME FIRST-HAND EXPERIENCE OF THE TRENCHES.

RIGHT, CHURCHILL, WE'LL POST YOU TO THE GUARDS DIVISION.

AT THE FRONT...

I MUST TELL YOU, MAJOR CHURCHILL, THAT WE WERE NOT CONSULTED ABOUT YOUR JOINING US.

I CAN'T HELP THAT, COLONEL. I SUGGEST WE MAKE THE BEST OF IT!

In spite of a cold reception Churchill set about his duties with enthusiasm and soon gained respect and admiration. Before long he was made Lieutenant Colonel in charge of the 6th Royal Scots Fusiliers.

ENEMY BOMBARDMENTS WERE FIERCE AND FREQUENT.

HEAVY BARRAGE BUILDING UP, SIR! WON'T YOU GO TO THE CELLAR?

NO, THE BACK ROOM WILL DO FOR ME!

A MINUTE LATER....

IN THE CELLAR...

BLIMEY! DIRECT HIT ON TOP. COLONEL CHURCHILL'S BOUGHT IT FOR SURE!

LET'S GET UP THERE!

ARE YOU ALL RIGHT, SIR?

PERFECTLY. WHAT A MESS THEY'VE MADE OF THE SITTING ROOM!

MONTHS LATER.

I HEAR THAT THE 6th ROYAL SCOTS ARE TO BE AMALGAMATED AND THAT YOU'VE LOST YOUR COMMAND, CHURCHILL.

I'LL SOON GET ANOTHER.

LISTEN, CHURCHILL. A MAN OF YOUR CALIBRE HAS NO RIGHT TO WASTE HIS TIME WAITING FOR A BULLET. YOUR PLACE IS WHERE YOUR COUNTRY NEEDS YOU MOST— AT HOME!

TO BE CONTINUED

The HAPPY WARRIOR

The true life story of
SIR WINSTON CHURCHILL

France, 1916. Lt. Colonel Churchill of 6th Royal Scots Fusiliers has lost his command because of his battalion's amalgamation with another unit. He is urged to leave the army and to return to the home front where his marked abilities may be used, once again, to help run the war.

TOLD BY CLIFFORD MAKINS
DRAWN BY FRANK BELLAMY

GOODBYE, CHURCHILL. WE ALL HOPE THAT YOU'LL RETURN TO WESTMINSTER AT THE EARLIEST OPPORTUNITY.

Churchill left the army and returned home to the political scene. In 1917 he was appointed Minister of Munitions to speed the flow of arms to the British Expeditionary Force.

THIS IS THE CRUCIAL STAGE OF THE WAR. WE MUST HAVE MORE TANKS, GUNS, SHELLS AND BULLETS — MORE OF EVERYTHING!

August 1918. The tide turned and the Germans retreated everywhere. British tanks, the evolution of which Churchill had encouraged, played a vital part in the Allied advance.

11 a.m. NOVEMBER 11th., 1918!

ARMISTICE!

LONDON. CHURCHILL LOOKED DOWN ON THE CROWDS.

WE'VE WON THE WAR!

PEACE! IT'S PEACE!

YES, WE'VE WON THE WAR ALL RIGHT! AND NOW WE MUST WIN THE PEACE!

TROUBLED YEARS FOLLOWED THE WAR AND CHURCHILL'S FORTUNES ROSE AND FELL...

1922 GENERAL ELECTION

I'VE LOST MY SEAT, MY PARTY AND MY APPENDIX!

1924 BACK AGAIN! CHANCELLOR OF THE EXCHEQUER

1926 GENERAL STRIKE WORKERS UNITE

NO TRAINS, BUSES, NEWSPAPERS! AND ALL THE WORKERS HAVE DOWNED TOOLS!

1929 GENERAL ELECTION AND FALL OF THE GOVERNMENT

LABOUR BACK IN POWER AGAIN! WHAT WILL YOU DO NOW, CHURCHILL?

KEEP THE OPPOSITION BENCHES WARM — AND BIDE MY TIME!

TO BE CONTINUED

The HAPPY WARRIOR

The true life story of
SIR WINSTON CHURCHILL

England, 1929. With the fall of the Conservative Government, Winston Churchill loses his office as Chancellor of the Exchequer. But his constituents have been faithful and he still keeps his seat in the House of Commons.

TOLD BY CLIFFORD MAKINS
DRAWN BY FRANK BELLAMY

WITH LABOUR IN POWER, CHURCHILL, THE COUNTRY WILL GO FROM STRENGTH TO STRENGTH!

I VERY MUCH DOUBT IT!

The Labour Government did not last long. In the midst of the world economic crisis of 1931 a coalition government was formed, but Churchill was not invited to join it.

CHURCHILL WAS AN INDUSTRIOUS WORKER AT HIS HOME, CHARTWELL,

AND A LONE WARNING VOICE AT WESTMINSTER.

THE DEMAND IS THAT GERMANY SHOULD BE ALLOWED TO REARM... DO NOT LET US DELUDE OURSELVES!

THREE YEARS LATER IN BERLIN...

HEIL HITLER!

HEIL HITLER!

OUR GLORIOUS FATHERLAND WILL TAKE ITS RIGHTFUL PLACE AT THE HEAD OF ALL NATIONS. WE WILL CONQUER EUROPE, ASIA, THE WORLD! THE HOUR IS AT HAND!

MARCH, 1936. GERMAN TROOPS RE-OCCUPY THE RHINELAND.

MARCH, 1938. INVASION OF AUSTRIA. HITLER ENTERS VIENNA.

MARCH, 1939. GERMAN CHANCELLERY, BERLIN.

AUSTRIA IS OURS, CZECHOSLOVAKIA IS OURS! NOW FOR POLAND, FRANCE AND ENGLAND!

BEWARE OF ENGLAND, FUEHRER.

ENGLAND, FIELD-MARSHAL KEITEL, HAS NO STOMACH FOR A FIGHT. YOU WILL SEE!

AUGUST, 1939. GENERAL IRONSIDE COMES FROM POLAND TO VISIT CHURCHILL.

A GERMAN INVASION IS EXPECTED HOURLY IN POLAND, BUT ARMY MORALE IS HIGH.

I FEAR THE WORST!

DAWN, SEPTEMBER 1st. VICIOUS AIR ATTACKS MARK THE...

GERMAN INVASION OF POLAND

BOMBING RAIDS O[...] FIVE [...]
MASS ATTACK O[...]

AFTERNOON, SEPTEMBER 1st. PRIME MINISTER CHAMBERLAIN SENDS FOR CHURCHILL.

WAR IS IMMINENT, WINSTON. I PROPOSE TO FORM A WAR CABINET IMMEDIATELY AND I WANT YOU TO JOIN IT.

TO BE CONTINUED

The HAPPY WARRIOR

1st September, 1939. After weeks of mounting tension throughout Europe, Germany invades Poland, whom Britain and France are solemnly pledged to help with all their might. War is imminent. Prime Minister Neville Chamberlain calls Winston Churchill to No. 10 Downing Street and invites him to join the War Cabinet.

TOLD BY CLIFFORD MAKINS
DRAWN BY FRANK BELLAMY

PRIME MINISTER, I WILL GIVE YOU ALL THE SUPPORT WITHIN MY POWER.

I MUST TELL YOU THAT WE ARE NOW AT WAR WITH GERMANY...

BBC

11·15 a.m. SEPTEMBER 3rd, 1939.

THE AIR RAID SIRENS — THERE THEY GO!

VERY PROMPT. TRUST THE GERMANS TO WASTE NO TIME!

Churchill returned as First Lord of the Admiralty to the very room he had quitted 25 years ago. He vigorously prosecuted the war at sea. But after the quick collapse of Poland, the Western Front was quiet. This period was known as the 'phoney' war. Then in the spring of 1940.

GERMAN CHANCELLERY, BERLIN.

THE TIME HAS COME TO WIN THE WAR IN THE WEST. THIS WILL BE DONE BY STRIKING TWO MORTAL BLOWS AT THE ENEMY...

APRIL 9th, 1940. GERMAN INVASION OF DENMARK AND NORWAY. THE GERMAN AND BRITISH NAVIES CLASH AT NARVIK.

THE GERMANS SUFFERED.....

... AND SO DID THE BRITISH.

MORTALLY WOUNDED, CAPTAIN WARBURTON-LEE IN H.M.S. HARDY ISSUES HIS LAST COMMANDS.

SIGNAL FLOTILLA— 'CONTINUE TO ENGAGE THE ENEMY'!

The Norway campaign went badly for Britain. Chamberlain faced great hostility in the House.

THE GREAT BLOW! MAY 10th, 1940. GERMANY ATTACKS ON THE WESTERN FRONT.

HOLLAND AND BELGIUM INVADED!

TO BE CONTINUED

The HAPPY WARRIOR

The true life story of
SIR WINSTON CHURCHILL

MAY, 1940!

The fighting in Norway is going against Britain although First Lord Winston Churchill is rightly proud of the Navy's successes in the battles at sea. But now, Prime Minister Chamberlain is rapidly losing support. Then, on 10th May, Germany strikes on the Western Front. The greatest war machine ever forged is turned on Holland, Belgium and Luxembourg.

TOLD BY CLIFFORD MAKINS
DRAWN BY FRANK BELLAMY

ARMOURED COLUMNS SURGED ACROSS THE FRONTIERS.....

...BOMBS RAINED DOWN ON DEFENCELESS CITIES.

DOWNING STREET...

SEE WHO THAT WAS?

YES — WINSTON CHURCHILL!

CHURCHILL JOINED THE PRIME MINISTER AND LORD HALIFAX.

THE CRISIS DEMANDS A NATIONAL GOVERNMENT. I CANNOT GAIN THE CONFIDENCE OF ALL PARTIES, AND SO I MUST RESIGN.

AS A MEMBER OF THE HOUSE OF LORDS I CANNOT DO JUSTICE TO THE ROLE OF PRIME MINISTER IN THIS WAR.

WELL, WINSTON, IT LOOKS LIKE YOU.

SO BE IT.

LATER THAT DAY AT BUCKINGHAM PALACE...

MR CHURCHILL, I WANT TO ASK YOU TO FORM A GOVERNMENT.

SIR, I WILL CERTAINLY DO SO.

MAY 13th. HOUSE OF COMMONS. THE NEW PRIME MINISTER.

WE ARE IN THE PRELIMINARY STAGES OF ONE OF THE GREATEST BATTLES IN HISTORY... I WOULD SAY TO THIS HOUSE AS I SAID TO THOSE WHO JOINED THIS GOVERNMENT — *I HAVE NOTHING TO OFFER BUT BLOOD, TOIL, TEARS AND SWEAT!*

CABINET MEETING, MAY 14th.

SEVENTH FRENCH ARMY

BELGIANS

B·E·F·

FIRST FRENCH ARMY

NINTH FRENCH ARMY

SECOND FRENCH ARMY

GRAVE NEWS FROM FRANCE! THE GERMANS HAVE BROKEN THROUGH AT SEDAN AND ARE CARRYING ALL BEFORE THEM!

EARLY NEXT MORNING...

SIR! MONSIEUR REYNAUD, THE FRENCH PRIME MINISTER, IS CALLING YOU FROM PARIS!

WE ARE DEFEATED! WE HAVE LOST THE BATTLE!

WHAT, SO SOON! I DON'T BELIEVE IT! I WILL FLY TO PARIS AT ONCE!

TO BE CONTINUED

The HAPPY WARRIOR

The true life story of SIR WINSTON CHURCHILL

May, 1940. Following the German attack on the Western Front, Winston Churchill becomes Prime Minister. As soon as he takes office, the mighty German army turns its full force against France and breaks the line at Sedan. The French Prime Minister calls Churchill on the telephone from Paris to say that the battle is all but lost.

TOLD BY CLIFFORD MAKINS
DRAWN BY FRANK BELLAMY

I MUST FLY TO PARIS! GENERALS DILL AND ISMAY SHALL GO WITH ME!

LE BOURGET AIRFIELD, PARIS...

WELL, HERE WE ARE!

PRAY GOD IT'S NOT TOO LATE!

QUAI D'ORSAY. FRENCH FOREIGN OFFICE.

HERE COMES WINSTON CHURCHILL.

WHAT HELP CAN HE BE TO FRANCE!

GENERAL GAMELIN, WILL YOU EXPLAIN THE SITUATION AT THE FRONT.

THE GERMANS HAVE BROKEN THROUGH NORTH AND SOUTH OF SEDAN ON A FRONT OF FIFTY MILES. THEY ARE RUSHING ON AT INCREDIBLE SPEED. OUR ARMIES ARE HOPELESSLY SHATTERED!

IMPOSSIBLE! WHAT ABOUT YOUR RESERVES? OU EST LA MASSE DE MANOEUVRE?

AUCUNE! -THERE IS NONE.

BACK IN LONDON THE FOLLOWING DAY...

GERMAN PANZER DIVISIONS ARE RAGING THROUGH FRANCE. THE BRITISH EXPEDITIONARY FORCE IS IN GRAVE PERIL. A LARGE SCALE EVACUATION MAY BE NECESSARY.

The Dutch army is shattered. Soon the Belgians surrender. The B.E.F., commanded by Lord Gort, fights a magnificent retreat to the sea. Meanwhile, Hitler exults in Berlin.

FUEHRER! GLORIOUS NEWS! THE FRENCH ARE CUT TO PIECES AND SOON THE BRITISH WILL BE HURLED INTO THE SEA!

VICTORY! VICTORY FOR THE FATHERLAND!

HEIL, HITLER!

WITH THE B.E.F. BEFORE DUNKIRK...

COME ON, LADS! FIRE OFF THE LOT AT THE BLIGHTERS, THEN WE'LL GO TO THE SEASIDE FOR THE DAY!

COR BLIMEY!

A QUIET LITTLE SPOT CALLED— DUNKIRK!

WE MUST MOVE HEAVEN AND EARTH TO EVACUATE THE ARMY FROM DUNKIRK. WE MUST SEND LIFEBOATS, DINGHIES, TRAWLERS, YACHTS — EVERYTHING AND ANYTHING THAT WILL FLOAT!

THE VAST ARMADA OF LITTLE SHIPS SET SAIL ACROSS THE CHANNEL.

WHATEVER HAPPENS AT DUNKIRK, WE SHALL FIGHT ON!

TO BE CONTINUED.

The HAPPY WARRIOR

The true life story of SIR WINSTON CHURCHILL

THE BEACHES OF DUNKIRK, MAY 30th, 1940

May, 1940. The fate of France is in the balance. German armoured columns are racing through the country. Everywhere the allied armies are in retreat. The British Expeditionary Force has fought its way to the sea. In Britain, Prime Minister Churchill is now securely at the helm. Then a great armada of little ships sails from our shores to evacuate the British Army from Dunkirk.

TOLD BY CLIFFORD MAKINS DRAWN BY FRANK BELLAMY

ALL ABOARD! ANY MORE FOR THE SKYLARK!

HERE COMES JERRY AGAIN!

YOU ALL RIGHT, SKIPPER?

NO, I'M DONE FOR! —NEVER MIND ME. GET THE LADS ON BOARD AND GET THEM HOME.

MIDNIGHT, JUNE 4th. THE FINAL PHASE. BRITISH REARGUARD IS EMBARKED.

THAT SAME DAY. HOUSE OF COMMONS.

WE SHALL DEFEND OUR ISLAND, WHATEVER THE COST MAY BE, WE SHALL FIGHT ON THE BEACHES, WE SHALL FIGHT ON THE LANDING GROUNDS, WE SHALL FIGHT IN THE FIELDS AND IN THE STREETS; WE SHALL FIGHT IN THE HILLS; *WE SHALL NEVER SURRENDER!*

I MUST FLY TO FRANCE AGAIN WITH SIR JOHN DILL.

IN FRANCE, RESISTANCE WAS ALMOST AT AN END.

ALLIED SUPREME WAR COUNCIL MEETS NEAR ORLEANS.

THERE IS NOTHING TO PREVENT THE ENEMY REACHING PARIS. OUR LAST LINE HAS BEEN BREACHED. THERE ARE NO RESERVES. *C'EST LA DISLOCATION —THE BREAK UP!*

THEY ARE BEATEN. THEY HAVE NO WILL TO RESIST.

THE GERMANS HAVE 100 DIVISIONS TO INVADE ENGLAND. WHAT WILL YOU DO WHEN THEY SWARM ACROSS THE CHANNEL?

DROWN AS MANY AS POSSIBLE —AND AS FOR THE OTHERS, WHEN THEY CRAWL ASHORE WE WILL *FRAPPER SUR LA TÊTE!*

TO BE CONTINUED.

The HAPPY WARRIOR

The true life story of
SIR WINSTON CHURCHILL

June, 1940. The German blitzkrieg on the Western Front has forced Holland and Belgium to surrender and shattered the French Army. The British Expeditionary Force has been evacuated from Dunkirk by thousands of little ships plying the Channel. Winston Churchill repeatedly crosses to France to inspire the French government to fight on. But at a meeting of the Allied War Council near Orleans, the French are ready to surrender.

TOLD BY CLIFFORD MAKINS
DRAWN BY FRANK BELLAMY

GOODBYE! THIS IS A DARK HOUR BUT I AM SURE WE WILL TRIUMPH IN THE END. EVEN IF FRANCE IS OCCUPIED WE WILL STILL WIN THE WAR.

WE SHALL SEE!

POOR CHURCHILL! IN A FEW WEEK'S TIME ENGLAND'S NECK WILL BE WRUNG LIKE A CHICKEN!

On 14th June, the Germans occupied Paris. M. Reynaud, the French Prime Minister, resigned and was succeeded by the aged Marshal Petain who made peace with Adolf Hitler.

IN LONDON...

WELL, THAT'S THAT! THE BATTLE OF FRANCE IS OVER — NOW FOR THE BATTLE OF BRITAIN!

WINSTON, YOU MUST SPEAK TO THE NATION AGAIN — WITHOUT DELAY.

HITLER KNOWS THAT HE WILL HAVE TO BREAK US IN THIS ISLAND OR LOSE THE WAR ... LET US, THEREFORE, BRACE OURSELVES TO OUR DUTIES AND SO BEAR OURSELVES THAT IF THE BRITISH EMPIRE AND ITS COMMONWEALTH LAST FOR A 1000 YEARS, MEN WILL STILL SAY *"THIS WAS THEIR FINEST HOUR"!*

MEANWHILE, THE NAZIS REJOICED ...

FUEHRER, WITH OUR BASES IN FRANCE THE LUFTWAFFE WILL SHOOT THE R.A.F. FROM THE SKIES!

AND THEN THE INVASION OF ENGLAND! NOTHING CAN STOP US NOW!

IN JULY, THE BATTLE OF BRITAIN BEGAN IN EARNEST. GREAT WAVES OF GERMAN BOMBERS WITH HEAVY FIGHTER ESCORTS CROSSED THE COAST IN DAYLIGHT RAIDS...

ACHTUNG! SPITFIRES!

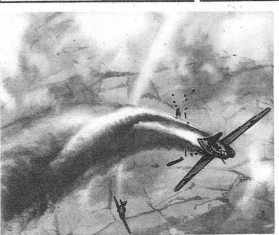

BIGGIN HILL AIRFIELD, KENT. ONE OF THE LEADING FIGHTER STATIONS.

WHAT A SHAMBLES!

LOOK, HERE COMES THE GRAND OLD MAN HIMSELF!

THEY'RE BASHING US ABOUT A BIT, SIR, BUT THEY CAN'T KEEP OUR PLANES OUT OF THE SKY!

THE FATE OF THE COUNTRY NOW RESTS WITH YOU — OUR FIGHTER PILOTS. GOD BE WITH ALL OF YOU!

TO BE CONTINUED.

The HAPPY WARRIOR

The true life story of SIR WINSTON CHURCHILL

August, 1940. The Battle of France is ended and the Battle of Britain is raging! Daily, great waves of German bombers with fighter escorts are launched against the defences and airfields of Southern England. Prime Minister Churchill visits the forward stations of Fighter Command as the great battle for air supremacy nears its climax . . .

TOLD BY CLIFFORD MAKINS
DRAWN BY FRANK BELLAMY

ALL No. 11 GROUP AIRFIELDS ARE BEING BOMBED INCESSANTLY.

ENEMY LOSSES ARE HEAVY — BUT SO ARE OURS. CAN WE REPLACE OUR LOST PLANES?

TAKE HEART! LORD BEAVERBROOK IS WORKING MIRACLES WITH THE AIRCRAFT INDUSTRY. THE LUFTWAFFE WILL NEVER RULE THESE SKIES!

GERMAN AIR ATTACKS BECAME BIGGER AND FIERCER . . . . .

THERE THEY ARE, CHAPS — DEAD AHEAD! NO MORE THAN 500 OF 'EM! HERE WE GO!

MEANWHILE, BOMBER COMMAND, WITH LIMITED RESOURCES, STRUCK BACK.

OUR BRITISH AIRMEN ARE TURNING THE TIDE OF THE WORLD WAR BY THEIR PROWESS AND DEVOTION... NEVER IN THE FIELD OF HUMAN CONFLICT HAS SO MUCH BEEN OWED BY SO MANY TO SO FEW!

AND HITLER RAGED IN BERLIN...

WE HAVE FAILED TO SHOOT THE R.A.F FROM THE SKIES — ON THE CONTRARY, THEY HAVE MORE PLANES THAN EVER! THE INVASION MUST BE POSTPONED. NOW LET OUR BOMBERS RAZE LONDON TO THE GROUND. WE WILL GIVE THAT WARMONGER CHURCHILL A LESSON! BOMB LONDON!

THE BLITZ!

EARLY IN SEPTEMBER, THE LUFTWAFFE SWITCHED THEIR ATTACKS TO LONDON. EVERY NIGHT THROUGHOUT THE AUTUMN AND THE WINTER BOMBS RAINED DOWN ON THE GREATEST CAPITAL CITY IN THE WORLD...

THE PRIME MINISTER WAS STILL AT No. 10 DOWNING STREET...

GET YOUR TIN HATS! WE'RE GOING ON THE ROOF!

PALL MALL IS BLAZING FROM END TO END!

GREAT SCOTT! WHAT A SIGHT!

WINSTON! COME ON DOWN, THIS IS NO TIME FOR YOU TO RISK YOUR NECK!

WE MUST FACE THE FACT THAT LONDON MAY BE UTTERLY DESTROYED. EVERYTHING THAT IS HUMANLY POSSIBLE MUST BE DONE TO PROTECT AND COMFORT THE BRAVE PEOPLE OF THIS GREAT CITY!

TO BE CONTINUED

The HAPPY WARRIOR

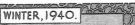

WINTER, 1940.

The massive daylight raids launched by German bombers and fighters throughout the summer have been defeated by the R.A.F.'s Spitfires and Hurricanes. Now the might of the Luftwaffe is turned on London and the great cities of Britain. Prime Minister Churchill, determined to stay at his post in Whitehall, sees large areas of London bombed and burned.

TOLD BY CLIFFORD MAKINS
DRAWN BY FRANK BELLAMY

NOT ONLY LONDON IS THREATENED WITH DESTRUCTION. THE WHOLE COUNTRY FACES A TERRIBLE ORDEAL. OUR GREAT CITIES WILL BE BOMBED INCESSANTLY. ANOTHER GRIM PHASE IS BEGINNING.

Night bombing raids were widespread. Coventry, Birmingham, Bristol, Southampton and Liverpool – these and many other towns and cities suffered heavily. Then, in December, came the fiercest of them all – the great fire raid on the City of London.

THE ANCIENT GUILDHALL WAS A SEA OF FLAMES...

FLEET STREET...

LOOK AT ST BRIDE'S – BLAZING LIKE A BONFIRE!

ST PAUL'S WILL BE THE NEXT TO GO!

ST PAUL'S ROSE MAJESTIC AMIDST FIRE AS THE CATHEDRAL WATCH FOUGHT TO SAVE THE GREAT CHURCH.

AND AT DAWN...

THANK GOD, THE OLD CHURCH IS STILL STANDING!

A MIRACLE.

GOOD OLD WINNIE!

WE CAN TAKE IT!

AND GIVE IT 'EM BACK!

WE WILL GIVE IT 'EM BACK ALL RIGHT! WE WILL REPAY THE DEBT TENFOLD, NAY, TWENTY FOLD. ALAS FOR POOR HUMANITY!

Meanwhile, the war spread across the world. In the Western Desert British troops, under Wavell, shattered the Italian Army, and the Italian Navy was badly mauled by the British Fleet. But Hitler was also active . . .

THE INVASION OF BRITAIN IS POSTPONED INDEFINITELY. WE MUST EXTEND THE WAR TO THE EAST!

FIRST THE BALKANS. WE MUST OCCUPY YUGOSLAVIA, BY FORCE IF NECESSARY, AND THEN CONQUER GREECE.

THEN WE SMASH THE BRITISH ARMY IN NORTH AFRICA. THIS MEANS WE HOLD SUEZ AND CONTROL THE MIDDLE EAST.

BUT, FUEHRER, IN THE WESTERN DESERT OUR ITALIAN ALLIES HAVE BEEN ROUTED!

PRECISELY! WE WILL GIVE THEM A STIFFENING OF GERMAN ARMOUR. I HAVE A FINE MAN FOR THE JOB – GENERAL ROMMEL!

LATER, IN LONDON...

WELL, WINSTON, WE'RE WEATHERING THE STORM ON THE HOME FRONT VERY WELL!

YES, BUT WE MUST NOW LOOK BEYOND THESE SHORES. GENERAL ROMMEL HAS ARRIVED IN AFRICA AND NAZI FORCES ARE CONCENTRATING IN THE BALKANS. THERE WILL BE BITTER FIGHTING SOON!

TO BE CONTINUED.

The HAPPY WARRIOR

The true life story of
SIR WINSTON CHURCHILL

Throughout the winter of 1940, London and the great towns of Britain have been bombed nightly by the Luftwaffe; but the people are still in good heart. Prime Minister Churchill, who has braved the blitz in Whitehall, now sees the war spreading. A German invasion of the Balkans seems imminent, and General Rommel has taken the Africa Corps to the Western Desert. Early in March, the British War Cabinet, together with the Chiefs of Staff, holds an urgent conference . . .

TOLD BY CLIFFORD MAKINS
DRAWN BY FRANK BELLAMY

IF WE AID GREECE WITH TROOPS FROM THE MIDDLE EAST, EGYPT WILL BE IN GRAVE PERIL.

A GREAT STRAIN WILL BE THROWN ON OUR FORCES IN THE DESERT.

WE MAY WELL FALL BETWEEN TWO STOOLS, AND YET . . .

AND YET OUR DUTY IS PLAIN. WE MUST STAND WITH THE GREEKS TO RESIST THE NAZIS, AND STILL FIGHT TOOTH AND NAIL IN THE WESTERN DESERT. THE WHOLE WORLD IS WATCHING US!

AND SO A GREAT PART OF THE ARMY OF THE NILE WAS SENT TO GREECE TO MEET THE THREATENED INVASION, AND THEN, IN THE WESTERN DESERT . . .

HERE COMES ROMMEL!

SPOILING FOR A FIGHT — AS USUAL!

ROMMEL'S PANZERS RACED ACROSS THE DESERT AND BEAT THE BRITISH BACK TOWARDS THE EGYPTIAN FRONTIER.

GENTLEMEN, THE FUEHRER EXPECTS US TO SWEEP THE BRITISH OUT OF CYRENAICA IN A MONTH'S TIME. WELL, WE WILL SURPRISE HIM — AND THE BRITISH ALSO. WE WILL ATTACK NOW!

AND AT GENERAL WAVELL'S DESERT H.Q . . .

ROMMEL HAS SURPRISED US! BUT HE CAN'T GO ON FOR EVER. WE MUST FORTIFY TOBRUK AND HOLD IT TO THE DEATH!

Meanwhile, powerful German forces invaded Yugoslavia and Greece. Within ten days, Yugoslavia capitulated. By the end of April, Greece too surrendered. British and Commonwealth troops were evacuated, leaving just in time . . .

WE HAVE BEEN BEATEN IN THE BALKANS AND HAMMERED HARD IN THE WESTERN DESERT — AND THERE MAY BE WORSE TO COME!

IT LOOKS LIKE IT, SIR! ALL OUR INTELLIGENCE CONFIRMS THAT AN ENEMY AIRBORNE INVASION OF CRETE IS CLOSE AT HAND.

LATER IN LONDON . . .

CRETE AND MALTA ARE VITAL TO US IN THE MEDITERRANEAN. WE HAVE 30,000 IMPERIAL TROOPS IN CRETE, WHICH MUST BE HELD AT ALL COSTS. GENERAL FREYBERG AND HIS NEW ZEALANDERS WILL NOT LET US DOWN!

MAY 20 1941
GERMAN AIRBORNE INVASION OF CRETE!

FOR PETE'S SAKE, JUST LOOK AT THOSE MUSHROOMS COMING DOWN!

LOVELY! WE'LL HAVE 'EM FOR BREAKFAST!

TO BE CONTINUED

The HAPPY WARRIOR

The true life story of
SIR WINSTON CHURCHILL

May, 1941. Britain is at bay in the Mediterranean area. Rommel's panzers have surged across the Libyan desert to the Egyptian frontier, and German armies have conquered Greece and Yugoslavia. Prime Minister Churchill urges the strongest resistance in the vital island of Crete, manned by 30,000 Imperial troops under the command of General Freyberg. In their bid to capture the island, the Germans launch the biggest-ever air assault . . .

TOLD BY CLIFFORD MAKINS. DRAWN BY FRANK BELLAMY.

HERE COME THE JERRIES AGAIN!

STAND FAST, LADS! WE'VE GOT TO STOP 'EM!

GET DOWN, CHAPS! FIGHTERS!

GENERAL FREYBERG'S H.Q., CRETE.

THEY'RE BOMBING US TO BLAZES, BUT WE'RE STILL HANGING ON, THANK GOD!

THE BRITISH FLEET WAS HEAVILY AND INCESSANTLY BOMBED OFF CRETE. H.M.S. WARSPITE WAS BADLY DAMAGED.

LONDON. CHURCHILL WATCHED THE COURSE OF EVENTS WITH GREAT FEELING.

IT LOOKS BLACK IN CRETE. THE ENEMY HAS ABSOLUTE CONTROL OF THE AIR.

IT'S A MOST VITAL BATTLE! THERE'S A GRAVE DANGER THAT THE MEDITERRANEAN FLEET MAY BE BADLY CRIPPLED BUT, IF WE STICK IT OUT, WE MAY YET WIN THE DAY!

TELEGRAPH FREYBERG: 'YOUR GLORIOUS DEFENCE COMMANDS ADMIRATION IN EVERY LAND. WE KNOW ENEMY IS HARD PRESSED. ALL AID IN OUR POWER IS BEING SENT.'

TO COMMANDERS-IN-CHIEF MIDDLE EAST: 'VICTORY IN CRETE ESSENTIAL AT THIS TURNING POINT IN THE WAR. KEEP HURLING IN ALL AID YOU CAN.'

ALAS, IT'S HOPELESS. OUR FRONT AT CANEA HAS COLLAPSED, OUR FORCES AT HERAKLION ARE SURROUNDED. WE MUST GET OUT—IF THERE'S TIME!

BUT, THAT VERY DAY, THE GALLANT FREYBERG WAS FORCED TO ADMIT DEFEAT.

IN LONDON . . .

IT IS THE END IN CRETE. WE HAVE LOST THE BATTLE. ANOTHER DEFEAT! ANOTHER WITHDRAWAL!

17,000 Imperial troops were evacuated from Crete, leaving behind 13,000 comrades, killed, wounded and captured. The Navy lost three cruisers and six destroyers. Meanwhile, the German battleship *Bismark* was sunk in the Atlantic. But Churchill faced a storm in the House . . .

IN VIEW OF THE OUTCOME, WHY WAS CRETE DEFENDED AT ALL? WAS IT NOT A LOST CAUSE? HAVE WE NOT SACRIFICED OUR MEN AND IMPERILLED OUR FLEET FOR NOTHING?

WHAT WOULD HAVE BEEN SAID IF WE HAD GIVEN UP THE ISLAND OF CRETE WITHOUT FIRING A SHOT? WE SHOULD HAVE BEEN TOLD THAT THIS PUSILLANIMOUS FLIGHT HAD SURRENDERED TO THE ENEMY THE KEY OF THE EASTERN MEDITERRANEAN!

TO BE CONTINUED.

The HAPPY WARRIOR

May, 1941. The great Battle of Crete has been fought and lost, but the Commonwealth troops have struck a mortal blow at German airborne power. The Fleet, though suffering serious losses, still controls the Mediterranean. But the defeat has caused concern in the House, and Prime Minister Churchill is forced to make an extensive review of the latest situation . . .

TOLD BY CLIFFORD MAKINS
DRAWN BY FRANK BELLAMY

I AM SURE IT WILL BE FOUND THAT THIS SOMBRE AND FEROCIOUS BATTLE OF CRETE . . . WAS WELL WORTH FIGHTING AND THAT IT WILL HAVE AN EXTREMELY IMPORTANT EFFECT ON THE WHOLE DEFENCE OF THE NILE VALLEY.

Churchill's masterly survey of the Battle of Crete completely re-assured the House. Meanwhile, in Berlin, Hitler was planning another colossal war . . .

BRITAIN MAY NOT BE BEATEN YET, BUT WE ARE THE MASTERS OF EUROPE—NOTHING CAN CHANGE THAT. NOW IS THE TIME TO STRIKE EAST — AT RUSSIA !

FUEHRER, IT IS A FEARFUL UNDERTAKING TO ATTACK RUSSIA.

WHY, WE HAVE ONLY TO KICK IN THE DOOR AND THE WHOLE ROTTEN STRUCTURE WILL COME TUMBLING DOWN. ONE SINGLE CAMPAIGN WILL SUFFICE !

JUNE 22nd, 1941

OPERATION BARBAROSSA !

GERMAN ATTACK ON RUSSIA. 164 DIVISIONS SUPPORTED BY 2,700 AIRCRAFT !

AS IN THE POLISH CAMPAIGN, THE LUFTWAFFE STRUCK SAVAGE BLOWS AT ALL AIRFIELDS.

ENGLAND. GENERAL DILL HURRIED DOWN TO CHEQUERS WITH DETAILED NEWS.

THE GERMANS HAVE ATTACKED ON A VAST FRONT AND ARE ADVANCING AT GREAT SPEED !

I EXPECTED IT ! I MUST BROADCAST TO THE NATION TONIGHT.

WE ARE RESOLVED TO DESTROY HITLER AND EVERY VESTIGE OF THE NAZI REGIME . . . . . . IT FOLLOWS, THEREFORE, THAT WE SHALL GIVE WHATEVER HELP WE CAN TO RUSSIA . . . . . . LET US REDOUBLE OUR EXERTIONS AND STRIKE WITH UNITED STRENGTH !

Within a month, the Germans were 300 miles into Russia. Great stores of British arms and supplies were sent to Russia. In the Western Desert, Auchinleck had replaced Wavell. Then, at a Cabinet meeting . . .

PRESIDENT ROOSEVELT HAS SUGGESTED THAT I MEET HIM IN NEWFOUNDLAND. I MOST EARNESTLY DESIRE THE CABINET'S APPROVAL OF THIS VENTURE, WHICH MUST SURELY BIND BRITAIN AND THE UNITED STATES CLOSER THAN EVER BEFORE.

EARLY IN AUGUST, THE PRIME MINISTER LEFT BRITAIN IN THE MIGHTY BATTLESHIP *PRINCE OF WALES*.

TO BE CONTINUED.

The HAPPY WARRIOR

The true life story of SIR WINSTON CHURCHILL

August, 1941. The power of the German war-machine is now at full blast. Following their conquest of Crete, the Nazis launch a gigantic offensive against Russia and, in a short time, advance hundreds of miles. Meanwhile, Prime Minister Churchill leaves Scapa Flow in the mighty battleship *Prince of Wales* to meet the President of the United States, Mr Roosevelt, at a secret rendezvous off Newfoundland . . .

TOLD BY CLIFFORD MAKINS
DRAWN BY FRANK BELLAMY

MAGNIFICENT! THIS IS A REAL HOLIDAY FOR ME!

I'M GLAD YOU'RE ENJOYING YOURSELF, MR CHURCHILL! I ONLY HOPE WE STEER CLEAR OF TROUBLE!

A FEW DAYS LATER...

WE'RE HERE –PLACENTIA BAY, NEWFOUNDLAND!

MR PRESIDENT!

PRIME MINISTER –IT'S GOOD TO SEE YOU!

STABLISH OUR HEARTS, O GOD, IN THE DAY OF BATTLE, AND STRENGTHEN OUR RESOLVE, THAT WE FIGHT NOT IN ENMITY AGAINST MEN BUT AGAINST THE POWERS OF DARKNESS ENSLAVING THE SOULS OF MEN!

SUNDAY, AUGUST 10th. DIVINE SERVICE FOR OFFICERS AND MEN OF THE BRITISH AND AMERICAN NAVIES ON BOARD THE *PRINCE OF WALES*.

Between them, the President and the Prime Minister devised the historic 'Atlantic Charter' which, in the name of Great Britain and the United States of America, gave suffering humanity hopes of a better world. Then Churchill sailed home to reflect on a terrible new menace which was brewing . . .

WE ARE FACING A NEW SERIOUS THREAT, IN THE FAR EAST. THERE IS EVERY INDICATION THAT JAPAN IS ABOUT TO ENTER THE WAR ON THE SIDE OF GERMANY AND ITALY. WE ARE GRIEVOUSLY UNDERMANNED IN THIS THEATRE AND SHALL DO WELL TO HOLD OUR OWN.

DECEMBER 7 1941

JAPANESE AIR ATTACKS ON PEARL HARBOUR HAWAII AND ON BRITISH POSSESSIONS IN MALAYA!

AT CHEQUERS, THE PRIME MINISTER'S COUNTRY RESIDENCE...

SIR, THE PRESIDENT OF THE UNITED STATES IS CALLING FROM WASHINGTON!

WE ARE WITH YOU TO THE END! GOD BE WITH YOU TOO! GOODBYE!

YES, IT'S TRUE ALL RIGHT. THE JAPANESE HAVE ATTACKED US AT PEARL HARBOUR AND CRIPPLED OUR FLEET! WE ARE ALL IN THE SAME BOAT NOW.

MEANWHILE, THE *PRINCE OF WALES* AND THE BATTLECRUISER *REPULSE* WERE SEEKING JAPANESE TRANSPORTS OFF MALAYA.

ENEMY AIRCRAFT APPROACHING!

WITHOUT AIR SUPPORT, THE TWO CAPITAL SHIPS FOUGHT A DESPERATE, LOSING BATTLE . . .

SOME HOURS LATER, AT THE ADMIRALTY...

SIR, TERRIBLE NEWS. WE HAVE LOST THE *PRINCE OF WALES* AND THE *REPULSE*.

GOOD GOD, WHAT A BITTER BLOW! I MUST PHONE THE PRIME MINISTER IMMEDIATELY.

TO BE CONTINUED.

The HAPPY WARRIOR

The true life story of SIR WINSTON CHURCHILL

The HAPPY WARRIOR

The true life story of
SIR WINSTON CHURCHILL

MAY, 1942

Britain and America are on the defensive before the on-slaught of Japan and the other Axis powers. Following the crippling of the U.S. fleet at Pearl Harbour, the great fortress of Singapore falls to the Japanese. Then Burma and the Dutch East Indies are occupied, and India and Australia are threatened. The whole British Empire is in grave peril, but Prime Minister Churchill is still undaunted and believes in ultimate victory . . .

TOLD BY CLIFFORD MAKINS
DRAWN BY FRANK BELLAMY

WHILE I HAVE THE CONFIDENCE OF THE BRITISH PEOPLE, I SHALL NEVER CONCEAL FROM THEM THE TRUTH ABOUT THE BLOWS WE ARE SUFFERING AND MUST GO ON SUFFERING.

MEETING OF THE WAR CABINET, LONDON.

WE MUST ATTACK AND DESTROY ROMMEL'S ARMY IN THE WESTERN DESERT. IT IS VITAL THAT GENERAL AUCHINLECK ATTACKS WITHOUT DELAY!

AUCHINLECK FEELS THAT OUR ARMY WILL HAVE THE BEST CHANCE IF ROMMEL ATTACKS FIRST.

I DON'T SHARE THAT VIEW AT ALL! WHILE ROMMEL IS GETTING READY, WE SHOULD HIT HIM —HARD!

WESTERN DESERT, A FEW WEEKS LATER — ROMMEL DID STRIKE FIRST!

WE HAVE WON THE DAY! THE BRITISH ARMOUR HAS BEEN ANNIHILATED. NOW WE WILL TAKE TOBRUK.

THE NEXT DAY, GERMAN TANKS PENETRATED THE DEFENCES OF TOBRUK . . .

MEANWHILE, CHURCHILL WAS IN WASHINGTON WITH PRESIDENT ROOSEVELT WHEN A TELEGRAM ARRIVED . . .

GEE—BAD NEWS FOR THE BRITISH! THIS SHOULD GO TO THE PRESIDENT'S ROOM IMMEDIATELY.

TOBRUK HAS SURRENDERED WITH 25,000 MEN TAKEN PRISONER.

WHAT CAN WE DO TO HELP?

MR PRESIDENT, GIVE US AS MANY SHERMAN TANKS AS YOU CAN SPARE AND SHIP THEM TO THE MIDDLE EAST, AS SOON AS POSSIBLE.

THIS IS THE MOMENT WHEN WE RISE OR FALL. I WILL FLY TO EGYPT MYSELF TO SIZE UP THE SITUATION — AND AFTER THAT I SHALL GO TO SEE STALIN IN MOSCOW.

CAIRO — A FEW DAYS LATER.

HERE COMES CHURCHILL'S 'PLANE. HE'S DONE IT AGAIN!

NOW WE SHALL SEE SOME FIREWORKS!

Churchill flew back to England, where he met uneasiness in the country and a storm in the House of Commons. But, following a great speech from the Prime Minister, a motion of no confidence was resoundingly defeated.

TO BE CONTINUED.

The HAPPY WARRIOR

The true life story of
SIR WINSTON CHURCHILL

For the time being, Japanese aggression in the Far East has been checked, and the Americans have won a great naval victory off Midway Island. But in the Western Desert, Rommel and his Africa Corps have won their biggest victory to date – the fortress of Tobruk has fallen and Egypt is menaced. Churchill flies to Egypt in order to make far-reaching decisions.

TOLD BY CLIFFORD MAKINS
DRAWN BY FRANK BELLAMY

WINSTON, WHEN WE GET TO THE EMBASSY, I ADVISE A SHORT REST.

CERTAINLY NOT – I'VE NEVER FELT BETTER! WE WILL GET STRAIGHT DOWN TO BUSINESS.

BRITISH EMBASSY, CAIRO. TWO DAYS LATER.

ROMMEL, ROMMEL, ROMMEL! WHAT ELSE MATTERS BUT BEATING HIM? WE MUST MAKE SWEEPING CHANGES IN OUR HIGH COMMAND.

After high-level discussions, in which General Smuts played a prominent part, General Auchinleck was relieved of his command. General Alexander replaced him, and General Montgomery was given command of the Eighth Army. Then Churchill set off for Moscow . . .

MOSCOW! I DOUBT IF WE SHALL GET A WARM RECEPTION HERE.

LATER, IN THE KREMLIN, FIERY DISCUSSIONS WITH STALIN TOOK PLACE.

THE BRITISH ARE AFRAID OF FIGHTING GERMANS! THEY SHOULD TRY IT SOME TIME, LIKE THE RUSSIANS – IT IS NOT TOO BAD!

BECAUSE OF THE BRAVERY OF THE RUSSIAN ARMY, I PARDON MR STALIN'S FOOLISH REMARKS – BUT HE IS TALKING NONSENSE.

AGREEMENT WAS REACHED IN THE END.

GOODBYE! TELL MR STALIN THAT I HAVE UNSHAKABLE FAITH IN THE TRIUMPH OF RUSSIA, BRITAIN AND AMERICA AGAINST OUR COMMON ENEMIES.

Churchill flew back to Cairo to meet Alexander and Montgomery. The great strategy for the defeat of Rommel was finally perfected. American intervention in Africa was to come a little later on. After visiting troops, the Premier flew home.

OCTOBER 23rd, 1942. GENERAL MONTGOMERY'S TACTICAL H.Q. IN THE WESTERN DESERT.

THE BATTLE WHICH IS NOW ABOUT TO BEGIN WILL BE ONE OF THE DECISIVE BATTLES OF HISTORY. IT WILL BE THE TURNING POINT OF THE WAR...THE LORD MIGHTY IN BATTLE WILL GIVE US THE VICTORY.

THE BATTLE OF ALAMEIN

ON A 7,000-YARD FRONT, NEARLY 1,000 GUNS OPENED FIRE.

AS THE BATTLE RAGED, HUGE BOMBING ATTACKS POUNDED ENEMY POSITIONS.

ROMMEL IS CRACKING! ONE GOOD, HARD BLOW AND HIS ARMY WILL BE FINISHED FOR EVER.

NOVEMBER 3rd. MONTGOMERY'S ARMOUR CRASHED THROUGH THE GERMAN LINES...

THEY'RE ON THE RUN, MATE – THEY'RE ON THE RUN!

TO BE CONTINUED.

The HAPPY WARRIOR

The true life story of SIR WINSTON CHURCHILL

OCTOBER — NOVEMBER, 1942
BATTLE OF ALAMEIN!

Following Churchill's visit to Cairo, sweeping changes are made in the Middle East Command. General Alexander replaces General Auchinleck as supreme commander, and General Montgomery is placed in command of the Eighth Army. Montgomery starts the Battle of Alamein with a stupendous artillery barrage. After several days of very bitter fighting, Rommel is put to flight . . .

TOLD BY CLIFFORD MAKINS
DRAWN BY FRANK BELLAMY

WE HAVE SMASHED THE GERMAN AND ITALIAN ARMY, AND SOON THE REMNANTS WILL BE PUSHED OUT OF EGYPT!

THE VICTORIOUS EIGHTH ARMY CHASED ROMMEL OUT OF EGYPT

GENERAL ALEXANDER, WITH HIS BRILLIANT COMRADE AND LIEUTENANT, GENERAL MONTGOMERY, HAS GAINED A GLORIOUS AND DECISIVE VICTORY.

GENERAL ROMMEL'S H.Q.

GENERAL ROMMEL, WE HAVE EIGHTY TANKS LEFT AGAINST SIX HUNDRED BRITISH!

IT IS THE END OF THE AFRICA CORPS! WE MUST KEEP ON RUNNING.

IF ONLY HITLER HAD GIVEN ME A FRACTION OF THE TROOPS HE HAS THROWN AGAINST RUSSIA, THE VICTORY WOULD HAVE BEEN OURS. STILL, WE MUST FIGHT WHILE WE CAN!

FIERCE RESISTANCE WAS MET AT ALGIERS, WHEN H.M.S. *BROKE* AND *MALCOM* TRIED TO LAND AMERICAN TROOPS IN THE HARBOUR.

AT ORAN, AN AMERICAN TASK FORCE WAS LANDED IN FACE OF STERN OPPOSITION. H.M.S. *RODNEY* PLAYED A LEADING PART IN THE BOMBARDMENT.

Meanwhile, on November 7th, a new front was opened in Africa. Powerful British and American forces commanded by General Eisenhower landed at many points in French North Africa.

WITH HITLER IN MUNICH...

WE WILL NOT YIELD! WE MUST POUR MORE TROOPS INTO AFRICA, AND WE MUST SEIZE THE FRENCH FLEET AT TOULON.

HERR FUEHRER, THE BRITISH AND AMERICANS ARE NOW FIRMLY ESTABLISHED IN AFRICA — MONTGOMERY IN THE EAST AND EISENHOWER IN THE WEST.

TOO LATE! THE FRENCH HAVE DESTROYED THEIR FLEET.

EARLY ON NOVEMBER 27th, GERMAN FORCES DASHED THROUGH UNOCCUPIED FRANCE, ONLY TO FIND THAT THE FRENCH FLEET HAD ALREADY BEEN SCUTTLED AT TOULON.

In the meantime, after the heroic defence of Stalingrad, Russian troops began to take the offensive along a vast front. All the world over, the initiative was slowly but surely passing to the allies.

NOVEMBER 29th. CHURCHILL BROADCASTS TO THE WORLD.

THE BRITISH PEOPLE HAVE PROVED THEY CAN STAND DEFEAT ...I SEE NO REASON AT ALL WHY WE SHOULD NOT SHOW OURSELVES EQUALLY RESOLUTE AND ACTIVE IN THE FACE OF VICTORY!

TO BE CONTINUED.

The HAPPY WARRIOR

The true life story of
SIR WINSTON CHURCHILL

With the dawn of 1943, the tide of war has turned in favour of the Allies. The Russians are on the offensive, the 8th Army has destroyed the Africa Corps and powerful Anglo-American forces have landed in French North Africa. Prime Minister Churchill is jubilant, as he ponders the next stage of the titanic struggle to liberate mankind . . .

TOLD BY CLIFFORD MAKINS
DRAWN BY FRANK BELLAMY

THE END IS IN SIGHT IN AFRICA. OUR NEXT MOVE IS MOST VITAL ! I MUST GO TO WASHINGTON AGAIN, TO TALK THINGS OVER WITH THE PRESIDENT.

WELL, THIS TIME YOU'RE NOT FLYING ! THOSE ARE DOCTOR'S ORDERS, AND YOU MUST STICK TO THEM.

ALL RIGHT — THE *QUEEN MARY* IS SAILING TO NEW YORK WITH A LOAD OF GERMAN PRISONERS — I'LL KEEP THEM COMPANY !

THE GIANT LINER, WITH CHURCHILL AND HIS STAFF ABOARD, RACED ACROSS THE ATLANTIC . . .

AT GENERAL ALEXANDER'S H.Q. IN NORTH AFRICA.

THE AXIS IS CRUMBLING EVERYWHERE ! WE SHALL SOON HAVE GOOD NEWS FOR WINSTON.

MEANWHILE, OFF TUNISIA, BRITISH AND AMERICAN FIGHTERS WROUGHT HAVOC WITH GERMAN AIR TRANSPORT.

A FEW DAYS LATER.

AFRICA IS REDEEMED ! NOW WE WILL STRIKE AT EUROPE WITH ALL OUR MIGHT.

TO THE PRIME MINISTER, WASHINGTON — 'SIR, IT IS MY DUTY TO REPORT THAT THE TUNISIAN CAMPAIGN IS OVER. ALL ENEMY RESISTANCE HAS CEASED. WE ARE MASTERS OF THE NORTH AFRICAN SHORES.'

JULY — AUGUST. INVASION AND CONQUEST OF SICILY.

Sicily

AND AT HITLER'S HEADQUARTERS IN EAST PRUSSIA . . .

HERR FUEHRER ! MUSSOLINI IS DEPOSED AND MARSHAL BADOGLIO HAS FORMED A NEW ITALIAN GOVERNMENT.

TRAITORS ! THEY WILL MAKE PEACE WITH BRITAIN AND AMERICA !

WE MUST BOLT THE BACK DOOR QUICKLY, POUR TROOPS INTO ITALY AND OCCUPY ROME !

SEPTEMBER ! INVASION OF ITALY ! AN ALLIED ARMADA SAILED INTO THE GULF OF SALERNO.

Italy soon surrendered, but a powerful German army gripped the country and offered stern resistance in the South to the invading Allies. Meanwhile, Churchill returned to England in the battle-cruiser *Renown* . . .

WE HAVE BITTEN 300 MILES OFF ITALY'S BOOT ! ITALY IS OUT OF THE WAR, BUT GERMANY WILL FIGHT TO THE END — AND IT WILL BE A BITTER END !

TO BE CONTINUED.

The HAPPY WARRIOR

The true life story of
SIR WINSTON CHURCHILL

OCTOBER, 1943

Anglo-American [...]
under the suprem[...]
mand of General [...]
hower, have co[...]
Sicily, invaded It[...]
advanced 300 mile[...]
But, although It[...]
surrendered, the G[...]
are in occupation[...]
fighting sternly. C[...]
knows that Germa[...]
not give in wit[...]
struggle, but is [...]
that victory for t[...]
world is now [...]

TOLD BY CLIFFORD MAKINS
DRAWN BY FRANK BELLAMY

CABINET MEETING. GERMANY AND JAPAN ARE IN RETREAT. THE INITIATIVE IS WITH THE ALLIES. WE MUST OPEN THE SECOND FRONT WITHOUT DELAY. RUSSIA IS GETTING VERY IMPATIENT.

WILL STALIN NEVER STOP GRUMBLING?

YOU LEAVE UNCLE JOE TO ME! I PROPOSE THAT PRESIDENT ROOSEVELT AND I MEET STALIN TO SEEK AGREEMENT ON A MASTER PLAN TO WIN THE WAR.

WHAT! OFF ON YOUR TRAVELS AGAIN!

A FEW WEEKS LATER, IN NOVEMBER, 1943, THE BIG THREE— CHURCHILL, ROOSEVELT AND STALIN— MET IN TEHRAN ...

IT IS AGREED THAT BRITISH AND AMERICAN TROOPS INVADE FRANCE IN 1944.

IN OVERWHELMING FORCE.

VERY WELL, BUT LET IT BE SOON. WE HAVE BEEN WAITING LONG ENOUGH!

AFTER THE CONFERENCE, CHURCHILL PAID A VISIT TO GENERAL EISENHOWER IN TUNISIA. THE PRIME MINISTER WAS BEGINNING TO FEEL THE STRAIN...

IT'S GREAT TO SEE YOU AGAIN, SIR!

I FEAR MY VISIT MAY BE PROLONGED. I'M COMPLETELY AT THE END OF MY TETHER.

SOME HOURS LATER...

THE PRIME MINISTER IS SERIOUSLY ILL WITH PNEUMONIA. I'M VERY WORRIED. ON NO ACCOUNT MUST HE BE MOVED.

AFTER A FEW DAYS...

WINSTON, I ABSOLUTELY FORBID YOU TO DO ANY WORK. YOU MUST STAY STILL AND KEEP QUIET!

IN THAT CASE, SEND IN MY DAUGHTER SARAH. SHE CAN READ TO ME!

"IT IS A TRUTH UNIVERSALLY ACKNOWLEDGED, THAT A SINGLE MAN IN POSSESSION OF A GOOD FORTUNE, MUST BE IN WANT OF A WIFE ..."

AND THE P.M. RESTED WHILE HIS DAUGHTER READ JANE AUSTEN'S 'PRIDE AND PREJUDICE' ALOUD TO HIM!

Churchill recovered, and returned home after a short convalescence. Vast machinery for the invasion was set in motion and Eisenhower appointed as Supreme Commander. But in Italy, in atrocious weather, the Allied armies came up against heroic German resistance at Monte Cassino ...

THE SHATTERED STREETS ECHOED WITH BATTLE DAY AND NIGHT.

MAN ALIVE—WE'VE BEEN THREE MONTHS IN THIS PERISHING PLACE!

WHAT A HELL-HOLE!

AERIAL AND ARTILLERY BOMBARDMENTS WERE OVERWHELMING, BUT STILL THE GERMANS HELD OUT.

AT GENERAL ALEXANDER'S H.Q.

WE HAVE THROWN THE WHOLE OF THE MEDITERRANEAN AIR FORCE AND THE SHELLS FROM 800 GUNS AT CASSINO — AND STILL THEY DEFY US!

AND IN LONDON.

GERMAN RESISTANCE AT CASSINO IS SIMPLY AMAZING. MEANWHILE, THE ROAD TO ROME IS BARRED!

TO BE CONTINUED.

The HAPPY WARRIOR

The true life story of SIR WINSTON CHURCHILL

The HAPPY WARRIOR

The true life story of SIR WINSTON CHURCHILL

OPERATION OVERLORD

Under this code name, the Allied Invasion of France has been fixed for 5th June, 1944. While the Germans fortify the Atlantic Wall on the French coast, the Allied armies gather in Southern England. Churchill tells King George VI that he plans to watch invasion operations from the cruiser *Belfast*. The King, fired by this idea, says he would like to go too.

TOLD BY CLIFFORD MAKINS
DRAWN BY FRANK BELLAMY

MAP ROOM, ADMIRALTY.

ADMIRAL RAMSAY, HIS MAJESTY WOULD VERY MUCH LIKE TO BE WITH ME ON THE *BELFAST* ON D-DAY.

HIS MAJESTY? I COULDN'T POSSIBLY SUPPORT SUCH AN IDEA! THE RISK IS TOO GREAT.

AH, WINSTON, IF THE RISK IS TOO GREAT FOR ME, THEN IT IS TOO GREAT FOR YOU.

BUT, SIR, I AM GOING AS MINISTER OF DEFENCE, IN THE EXERCISE OF MY DUTY!

But the King agreed to stay at home, and soon afterwards persuaded Churchill to do likewise. And now D-Day, 5th June, was close at hand – but the weather forecast was gloomy.

H.Q. GENERAL EISENHOWER, SUPREME COMMANDER ALLIED EXPEDITIONARY FORCES, EARLY MORNING JUNE 4th, 1944.

IN FOUR HOURS' TIME, WE CAN EXPECT RISING WINDS AND THICK, LOW CLOUDS.

WE SHOULDN'T CHANCE A LANDING UNDER THOSE CONDITIONS.

AIR OPERATIONS WILL BE SEVERELY CURTAILED.

AT THIS STAGE, DELAY MIGHT BE FATAL. I THINK WE SHOULD GO!

NO, NO! I THINK WE MUST WAIT— THE ATTACK MUST BE POSTPONED. WE MUST HOPE AND PRAY THAT THE WEATHER WILL IMPROVE IN THE NEXT TWENTY-FOUR HOURS.

WELL, THERE IT IS – THE WEATHER'S STILL NOT GOOD, BUT IT HAS IMPROVED A LITTLE. IF WE DON'T GO TOMORROW, WE WILL HAVE TO CANCEL THE WHOLE SHOW FOR A FORTNIGHT.

A FEW HOURS LATER, CHURCHILL HEARD THE NEWS...

THIS IS IT, WINSTON! EISENHOWER HAS DECIDED TO GO TOMORROW.

AND SO THE DIE IS CAST!

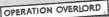

D-DAY June 6th, 1944

THE GREATEST INVASION IN HISTORY!

FIVE SPEARHEADS FORMED THE ASSAULT PLAN.

UTAH OMAHA GOLD JUNO SWORD

GREAT WAVES OF LANDING-CRAFT AND WARSHIPS AND AIRCRAFT BORE DOWN ON THE NORMANDY BEACHES.

THEN THE ASSAULT!

WELL, MATES, WE'RE HERE!

'AND GENTLEMEN IN ENGLAND NOW A'BED SHALL THINK THEMSELVES ACCURS'D THEY WERE NOT HERE!'

COR BLIMEY! 'ARK AT 'IM!

PARATROOPERS WERE DROPPED BEHIND THE GERMAN LINES.

HUNDREDS OF WARSHIPS BOMBARDED THE COAST.

TROOPS UNDER FIRE DASHED FROM THEIR LANDING-CRAFT.

TO BE CONTINUED.

The HAPPY WARRIOR

The true life story of
SIR WINSTON CHURCHILL

TOLD BY CLIFFORD MAKINS
DRAWN BY FRANK BELLAMY

June, 1944 — Second Front in Europe! On 6th June, a vast armada of ships carrying huge forces of British, Imperial and American troops crossed the Channel to assault the Normandy beaches, on the French coast. In spite of fierce resistance, successful landings are made everywhere. At noon on the same day, Prime Minister Churchill tells of these achievements to a crowded House of Commons...

AN IMMENSE ARMADA OF UPWARDS OF 4,000 SHIPS HAS CROSSED THE CHANNEL. MASSED AIRBORNE LANDINGS HAVE BEEN SUCCESSFULLY EFFECTED. THE FIRE OF SHORE BATTERIES HAS BEEN LARGELY QUELLED.

FOUR DAYS LATER...

MONTGOMERY REPORTS THAT HE'S WELL ENOUGH ESTABLISHED ON SHORE FOR US TO PAY HIM A VISIT.

SPLENDID! WE'LL GO RIGHT AWAY.

THE TIRELESS PREMIER WENT TO FRANCE.

WELCOME TO FRANCE, SIR!

THIS IS A GREAT MOMENT FOR US ALL! NOW, PLEASE MAY WE SEE THE SIGHTS!

GOOD OLD WINNIE!

WE HAVE PENETRATED ABOUT EIGHT MILES INLAND. THE TROOPS ARE IN FINE FETTLE.

Churchill returned to London, confident that the Allied campaign was well under way. Then, suddenly, the citizens of London were subjected to yet another ordeal...

THE FLYING BOMB!

FLYING BOMBS WERE LAUNCHED FROM SITES IN NORTHERN FRANCE...

CROSSED THE CHANNEL AT 400 MILES PER HOUR...

AND EXPLODED IN LONDON.

CABINET MEETING.

LONDON IS SUFFERING BADLY FROM THESE 'DOODLE-BUGS'!

EXTENSIVE PLANS TO DESTROY THEM WILL SOON COME INTO FORCE.

BUT SHOULD WE CHANGE OUR STRATEGY IN FRANCE TO MEET THIS NEW THREAT?

NO, THAT IS JUST WHAT HITLER IS HOPING FOR. OUR STRATEGY REMAINS UNCHANGED. SOON WE WILL BREAK OUT OF NORMANDY AND CAPTURE THE FLYING BOMB SITES. MEANWHILE, LONDON CAN TAKE IT!

HITLER'S H.Q., MARGIVAL, FRANCE.

HERR FUEHRER, FIELD MARSHALS RUNSTEDT AND ROMMEL HAVE ARRIVED.

SEND THEM IN.

OUR ARMIES ARE BLEEDING TO DEATH IN NORMANDY. WE SHOULD WITHDRAW TO THE SEINE AND FIGHT THERE.

THE ALLIED AIR FORCES OVERWHELM US NIGHT AND DAY. IT IS TERRIFYING!

NO-NO! THERE MUST BE NO RETREAT. THE ARMY MUST FIGHT AND DIE WHERE IT STANDS. OUR FLYING BOMBS WILL SOON BRING BRITAIN TO HER KNEES!

EARLY JULY. THE DECISIVE BATTLE OF CAEN...

ONCE CAEN IS CAPTURED, THE WAY INTO FRANCE IS WIDE OPEN. A GREAT BATTLE FOR THIS CITY IS NOW NEARING ITS CLIMAX.

TO BE CONTINUED

The HAPPY WARRIOR

The true life story of
SIR WINSTON CHURCHILL

JULY, 1944!

One month after the Normandy invasion, the Allies have a firm foothold in France. But the Germans are resisting bitterly, and the Allies have not yet broken out from their limited positions. In London, flying bombs explode as Mr Churchill awaits the outcome of the crucial battle of Caen, which Montgomery is fighting with British and Canadian troops.

TOLD BY CLIFFORD MAKINS
DRAWN BY FRANK BELLAMY

ON JULY 10th, BRITISH TROOPS WERE MOPPING UP IN THE RUINS OF CAEN.

SUDDENLY, OUT OF THE RUINS...

BLIMEY! HERE'S A 'TIGER'—STILL INTACT! WHAT A WHOPPER!

BACK A BIT, LADS — THE ANTI-TANK BOYS CAN DEAL WITH THIS ONE!

WAIT FOR IT ...FIRE!

GOT HIM!

LONDON, THE NEXT DAY...

MONTGOMERY HAS WON THE BATTLE OF CAEN. BEFORE THE NEXT BIG OFFENSIVE STARTS, I THINK I'LL PAY ANOTHER VISIT TO THE FRONT.

CHURCHILL WENT TO ARROMANCHES, TO SEE THE WORK OF THE PREFABRICATED MULBERRY HARBOUR WHICH HE HAD INSPIRED LONG AGO...

THE MULBERRY IS GOING GREAT GUNS, SIR. THE LORD KNOWS WHAT WE WOULD HAVE DONE WITHOUT IT!

THE WORK YOU HAVE DONE HERE IS NOTHING SHORT OF MIRACULOUS.

Soon the Allies were sweeping through France. In the South, the American General Patton's army shot forward at amazing speed, and reached the Seine in August. In the North, British and Canadian troops struck towards Belgium and Holland.

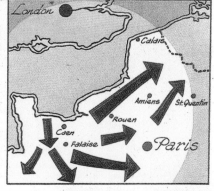

HOUSE OF COMMONS, SEPTEMBER.

NOT ONLY PARIS, BUT PRACTICALLY THE WHOLE OF FRANCE HAS BEEN LIBERATED. BELGIUM HAS BEEN RESCUED—PART OF HOLLAND IS ALREADY FREE — THE ALLIED ARMIES HAVE REACHED THE GERMAN FRONTIERS.

WELL, WINSTON, IT LOOKS AS IF THE WAR WILL BE OVER BY CHRISTMAS!

AH, MY FRIEND, I SHOULDN'T COUNT ON THAT AT ALL. WE HAVE CORNERED THE BEAST IN HIS DEN, BUT HE IS STILL DANGEROUS AND MIGHT SPRING AT ANY MOMENT.

AND AT HITLER'S H.Q...

THE ALLIED ARMIES ARE KNOCKING AT THE GATES OF GERMANY. VERY WELL! I HAVE PLANNED AN ATTACK WHICH WILL SPLIT THEM IN TWO AND SEND THEM REELING BACK TO THE SEA!

TO BE CONTINUED.

The HAPPY WARRIOR

The true life story of
SIR WINSTON CHURCHILL

OCTOBER, 1944.

The victorious Allied Armies have reclaimed France, and most of Holland and Belgium, from the Germans. But now, after this great victory, the offensive has come to a halt. Prime Minister Churchill emphasizes that much hard fighting lies ahead. Meanwhile, Hitler is planning a last, desperate assault in an effort to save the day for Germany.

TOLD BY CLIFFORD MAKINS
DRAWN BY FRANK BELLAMY

WE WILL LAUNCH A COUNTER-ATTACK IN THE ARDENNES EARLY IN DECEMBER. OUR OBJECTIVE IS THE RECAPTURE OF ANTWERP.

A BOLD PLAN INDEED, MEIN FUEHRER!

BUT WE HAVEN'T THE MEN, THE MACHINES — WE HAVEN'T THE PETROL!

I WILL NOT LISTEN TO DEFEATIST TALK! THE ATTACK WILL TAKE PLACE AS PLANNED. THE AMERICAN ARMIES WILL BE CUT IN TWO AND THE BRITISH ARMY ISOLATED. WAIT AND SEE!

O.K., FELLAS — THEY'RE COMING RIGHT AT US. NOW GIVE 'EM A ROUSING WELCOME!

THE GERMANS GATHERED STRENGTH AND, IN DECEMBER, STRUCK HARD IN THE ARDENNES...

BUT THE GERMAN COLUMNS SURGED ON.

AND IN LONDON...

THE GERMANS HAVE BROKEN THROUGH, ALL RIGHT — FIERCE FIGHTING AND CONFUSION EVERYWHERE.

I DO NOT THINK THEY WILL GET FAR. I WILL SPEAK TO EISENHOWER TONIGHT.

IT'S TOUGH GOING, BUT WE WILL HOLD THEM. I HAVE BRADLEY IN CHARGE IN THE SOUTH AND MONTGOMERY IN THE NORTH.

SPLENDID! BRITISH TROOPS WILL ALWAYS DEEM IT AN HONOUR TO ENTER THE SAME BATTLE AS THEIR AMERICAN FRIENDS.

The Ardennes battle was severe, but superb fighting qualities of American and British soldiers prevailed. By the end of January, 1945, the Germans were driven back with huge losses. Meanwhile, Russian armies were rolling through Poland in the East, and the Allies prepared their final assault on Hitler in the West.

CABINET MEETING, MARCH, 1945.

THE ALLIED ARMIES ARE ABOUT TO CROSS THE RHINE. I WANT TO BE WITH THE BRITISH ARMY AT THE CROSSING.

WINSTON, THESE TRIPS WILL BE THE DEATH OF YOU.

FIELD MARSHAL MONTGOMERY'S HEADQUARTERS, NEAR VENLO...

WE WILL FORCE THE RIVER AT TEN POINTS ON A TWENTY MILE FRONT. IN THE EARLY STAGES, TWO AIRBORNE DIVISIONS WILL BE DROPPED.

AH! I MUST SEE THAT!

NEXT DAY — *THE MIGHTY ATTACK WAS LAUNCHED. 2,000 PLANES TOOK PART IN THE ASSAULT, AND DROPPED 14,000 MEN WITH ARTILLERY AND ARMS...*

THERE THEY GO. AT LAST THE FULL FORCE OF WAR HAS COME TO GERMANY. THE END OF AN AWFUL TYRANNY IS AT HAND.

TO BE CONTINUED

The HAPPY WARRIOR

The true life story of
SIR WINSTON CHURCHILL

HERE COMES WINSTON AGAIN! FOR A PRIME MINISTER, HE SURE GETS AROUND!

MY DEAR GENERAL, THE GERMAN IS WHIPPED, WE'VE GOT HIM! HE IS ALL THROUGH!

March, 1945! Following the failure of the German counter-attack in the Ardennes, the Allied armies make their great assault across the Rhine into Germany. Churchill has watched the initial phases of the battle in the North with Field Marshal Montgomery. Then, as the attacks meet with success, the Premier pays a visit to the Supreme Allied Commander, General Eisenhower.

TOLD BY CLIFFORD MAKINS
DRAWN BY FRANK BELLAMY

ALLIED TROOPS SWARMED INTO GERMANY ACROSS FLOATING BRIDGES THROWN ACROSS THE RHINE. GERMANY'S WEST FRONT HAD COLLAPSED!

THE ALLIED ARMIES ARE ADVANCING INTO THE HEART OF GERMANY. THE GREAT GERMAN ARMY IS BREAKING UP. THOUSANDS HAVE LAID DOWN THEIR ARMS. VICTORY IS AT HAND!

Then, at the hour of triumph...

PRESIDENT ROOSEVELT IS DEAD

FRANKLIN ROOSEVELT WAS THE GREATEST AMERICAN FRIEND WE HAVE EVER KNOWN, AND THE GREATEST CHAMPION OF FREEDOM WHO HAS EVER BROUGHT HELP AND COMFORT FROM THE NEW WORLD TO THE OLD.

NOW THE FALL OF GERMANY WAS IMMINENT. THE ARMIES OF THE WESTERN ALLIES WERE ABOUT TO MEET THE ARMIES OF RUSSIA...

WELL, I SHALL STAY HERE AND DIE. TELL THE PEOPLE THAT THEIR FUEHRER IS IN BERLIN AND WILL REMAIN HERE TO THE END. THAT IS MY LAST WORD!

THE REICH CHANCELLERY WAS BURNING...

AND IN THE SHELTER BENEATH THE CHANCELLERY...

MEIN FUEHRER, ALL IS LOST! BERLIN IS DOOMED. GET OUT WHILE THERE IS STILL TIME. IT IS DEATH TO STAY HERE!

...AND THE FOCAL POINT WAS *BERLIN!*

TO BE CONTINUED.

The HAPPY WARRIOR

The true life story of **SIR WINSTON CHURCHILL**

APRIL, 1945

Assailed from East and West, the German Army has crumbled and the defeat of the Third Reich is imminent. President Roosevelt is dead, and Mussolini murdered by partisans. Churchill is triumphant. In doomed Berlin, Hitler has decided to take his life as the Russians invade the German capital and near the city's centre.

TOLD BY CLIFFORD MAKINS
DRAWN BY FRANK BELLAMY

THE RUSSIANS HAVE OCCUPIED THE TIERGARTEN ~ THEY ARE ONLY A FEW BLOCKS AWAY!

NO MATTER—THE FUEHRER IS DEAD.

ON APRIL 30th, WITH RUSSIAN SHELLS FALLING ALL AROUND, HITLER'S BODY WAS BURNED IN THE CHANCELLERY GARDENS AND NO TRACE OF IT WAS EVER FOUND.

MAY 2nd 1945

END OF WAR IN ITALY

NEARLY A MILLION GERMANS SURRENDER

MAY 7th 1945

END OF WAR IN GERMANY
JODL SIGNS INSTRUMENT OF UNCONDITIONAL SURRENDER

WITH THIS SIGNATURE, THE GERMAN PEOPLE AND THE GERMAN ARMED FORCES ARE, FOR BETTER OR FOR WORSE, DELIVERED INTO THE VICTOR'S HANDS...

MAY 8th 1945

CHURCHILL SPEAKS TO THE NATION...

THE GERMAN WAR IS AT AN END. OUR GRATITUDE TO ALL OUR SPLENDID ALLIES GOES FORTH FROM ALL OUR HEARTS. ADVANCE BRITANNIA! LONG LIVE THE CAUSE OF FREEDOM! GOD SAVE THE KING!

...THEN DRIVES TO THE HOUSE THROUGH CHEERING CROWDS...

GOOD OLD WINNIE!

GOD BLESS HIM!

THE HOUSE RISES TO HIM...

HIP HIP HOORAY!

FOR HE'S A JOLLY GOOD FELLOW...

AND SO SAY ALL OF US!

AND, AFTER HIS SHORT ADDRESS, THE PRIME MINISTER CALLS THE HOUSE TO PRAYER.

I MOVE THAT THIS HOUSE DO NOW ATTEND AT THE CHURCH OF ST. MARGARET, WESTMINSTER, TO GIVE HUMBLE AND REVERENT THANKS TO ALMIGHTY GOD FOR OUR DELIVERANCE FROM THE THREAT OF GERMAN DOMINATION.

The war with Germany was over, but the war with Japan was still to be won. At once the Labour Party pressed for a General Election. On May 23rd, the Coalition Government was dissolved. After a strenuous election campaign, polling took place on July 5th. Ballot boxes remained sealed until service-men stationed overseas had recorded their votes.

THE VOTES WERE COUNTED ON JULY 25th...

SIR, THE FIRST RESULTS ARE COMING IN. THE SOCIALISTS ARE MAKING GREAT HEADWAY.

AH, I HAD A PREMONITION OF THIS!

NEVER MIND— IT MAY WELL BE A BLESSING IN DISGUISE.

WELL, IT'S QUITE CLEAR THAT THE SOCIALISTS WILL HAVE A LARGE MAJORITY. I'M OUT!

TO BE CONTINUED.

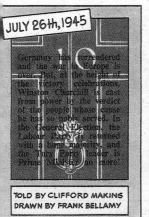

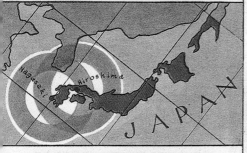

'Whom neither shape of danger can dismay,
Nor thought of tender happiness betray;
Who, not content that former worth stand fast,
Looks forward, persevering to the last...
And, while the mortal mist is gathering, draws
His breath in confidence of Heaven's applause:
This is THE HAPPY WARRIOR.'

WILLIAM WORDSWORTH